The Stone People

Sarah Wellington

PublishAmerica
Baltimore

© 2008 by Sarah Wellington.
All rights reserved. No part of this book may be reproduced, stored in a retrieval system or transmitted in any form or by any means without the prior written permission of the publishers, except by a reviewer who may quote brief passages in a review to be printed in a newspaper, magazine or journal.

First printing

All characters in this book are fictitious, and any resemblance to real persons, living or dead, is coincidental.

PublishAmerica has allowed this work to remain exactly as the author intended, verbatim, without editorial input.

ISBN: 1-60610-702-X
PUBLISHED BY PUBLISHAMERICA, LLLP
www.publishamerica.com
Baltimore

Printed in the United States of America

Acknowledgments

I want to thank Autumn Rivers for seeing through my ideas and editing them into a story that was readable. She has been invaluable to me on this book. The Stone People is dedicated to God. For without him it could not be possible.

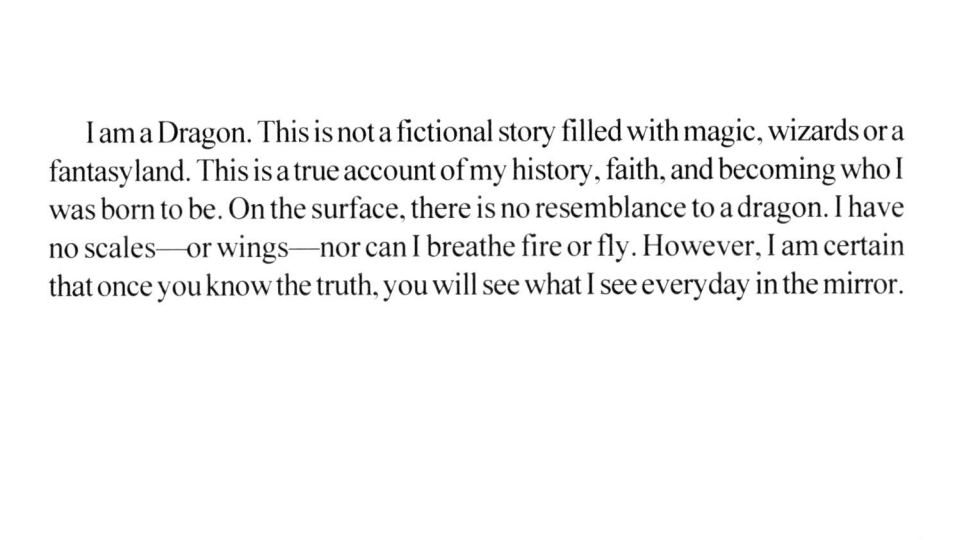

I am a Dragon. This is not a fictional story filled with magic, wizards or a fantasyland. This is a true account of my history, faith, and becoming who I was born to be. On the surface, there is no resemblance to a dragon. I have no scales—or wings—nor can I breathe fire or fly. However, I am certain that once you know the truth, you will see what I see everyday in the mirror.

Chapter One: Burn Day

    Northern California is a beautiful place to grow up as a child, as the climate is versatile enough to enlighten any young girl's imagination. Vacaville was the town where my grandfather's farm was located. Throughout my childhood, we lived in many places, but Locke Road would always be my home.

    Grandpa was a small farmer, he grew just enough to support his family and their children. We all put some work into the farm, whether the job is building a garage, raising a barn or simply feeding the animals. The work was hard, especially as the sun beat down each day, but-as a result, we learned the value of hard labor. In the end, the rewards always outweighed the hard work.

    My grandfather taught me everything I know about horses, from riding, to care, to good ol'e fashioned mucking out the stalls. One of the most important lessons was how to land in a pile of horseshit rather than on the hard earth. I would spend time everyday brushing, walking and feeding the horses, but my favorite activity was lying out while she grazed. Saucy was her name, a temperamental mare that preferred to eat instead of running. For that reason alone, she was my kind of horse.

    My brother and I awoke early in the morning for years to go and feed the animals, putting on our mud boots and robes over pajamas. The sun was often not up yet but we would trudge down to the barn, sleep still in our eyes. After breaking pieces of hay off the bale in order to feed the horses and the bull, we then threw out to the field for the cows. The pigs received two cans of feed, later getting the slop of leftovers from dinner and breakfast. Then it was off to the chicken coop for corn and egg collecting.

    Often the silence was beautiful, a quiet understanding we shared on the walk back to the trailer. Some mornings the air hung heavily with the unspoken events. A sigh escaped his lips.

"I hate this." Steve said. He offered no explanation, but there was no need. We both knew.

"Yeah, I don't like it either but it will change; that's what grandma always says." I did not look at him but I could hear the hope in his voice.

"Do you really think it will stop now that grandma and grandpa know too?" Thank God for the dark morning. It hid my eyes.

"Absolutely, the only person he fears is Grandpa, right?" Half hoping to believe the words that came so easily from my lips, he replied, "Oh yeah!" He does."

Steve seemed filled with a new hope. I swear I saw him skip to the stairs. I wished I could skip too.

That Saturday was burn day. We always took care of our refuse by burning. That which could not be recycled, burned, or eaten by the animals we hauled out on trash day. Grandpa would have Uncle Joe gather scraps; allowing us to help with that part. A big fifty-gallon drum like the kind for toxic waste, we used to burn the brush.

The kids usually went to go play when the actual burning took place but on this Saturday Grandpa asked me to stay. I was shocked but so ecstatic to help that I shortly forgot the last few days of a living hell.

~Wednesday~

"Before you gather to leave, I want your homework on my desk." Mrs. Devereaux stated just as the bell rang. The shuffling of books and papers were the harmony to the yelling and laughing. Much like Pavlov's dog, third-graders often become maniacs at the sound of a bell. I gathered my stuff and put away my pencils.

We had those lift-up desks then. I always liked those, as it felt like I had my own private desk. Mrs. Devereaux was my new favorite teacher. She was tall and regal-looking, with blonde hair, and constantly dressed in either long skirts or full-length dresses.

We had a coat closet in the classroom toward the back opposite of the door. I headed that way to get my coat and lunch box. A boy stood there already getting his things, too. Most of the class had already cleared out, eager for playtime. He was a black boy about head shorter than I was. It may seem petty to mention the color of his skin but that is all I remember. I do not even know his name. Whether he did or said something, I do not remember either. All I do know is that Mrs. Devereaux was at the front of the room talking with a student, and the rest of the classroom was deserted.

Me? Where was I? Not sure of what was going on; I awoke to find myself straddling the boy. I was throwing my whole body into punching him. He was crying and attempting to cover his face. Strangely enough, I do not remember the look on his face, but I do remember what I felt.

Rage…Pent up rage coursed through my veins.

I seemed to release each emotion with every fist that met some part of his body. Anger boiled within me, rehashing that pent-up fear and despair.

The classroom door opened and he walked in. I felt him before I heard him. In slow motion I turned. To a third grader he was a giant, but in my eyes, he was bigger than a giant was. Mrs. Devereaux seemed to take in the scene at the same moment. She pulled me off the boy I was beating. He said nothing to me, but the look was enough to let me know. It had happened before and would happen again. Mrs. Devereaux stood there talking to him. I understood nothing, only able to shake as I tried to steady myself.

I could not allow any anger to show. He could not see that. I knew instinctively that whatever waited for me would be worse if he saw that I was angry. Wordlessly, I followed him to the car. There would be no help from anywhere, even though I looked back to see if she would. The teacher however was attending to the boy whom I had spent three minutes pummeling.

They say the longest walk is the last mile. Sitting in the car, I could feel that trepidation, scared and numb all at the same time. I willed the ride home to be slow, hoping maybe an accident would occur and slow us down.

He was talking; rarely did he raise his voice. I almost missed that. The low, barely audible hiss that came out vibrated with hatred. Was I such a disappointment? Could he really hate me so much?

Wham!

My head crashed into the side of the door. The pain was a welcome explosion. We had an old car with no automatic door locks, and the lever was in the up position. Metal. Everything was metal. I did not feel it hit me but the window; I felt that.

I registered the question then; I missed it before. That was why he hit me. I really must pay closer attention.

"What in the hell were you thinking? Are you stupid? What must I do to get it through your fucking head?"

It was always the same, always. As usual, I did not have an answer.

"I don't know."

Wham!

My head crashed back into the window, the pain a welcome diversion. He hated those three words the most. I never could give him the right answer.

"You just wait until we get home." the low voice spat out. The silence cut through us again. He turned down our road, past the country store where I had spent my lunch money on candy. I found myself wishing I could go back to that morning to redo the day. Then none of this would be happening. We would be pulling into the store instead, to buy an ice cream, my reward for acing my pre-spelling test. That would be just a normal father/daughter outing.

The longest mile was indeed the last one as I turned back toward the road, waiting.

I remember praying for him to forget why he was angry. More so, I prayed for death. In fact, I welcomed the thought of oblivion then. With no other outlet, I turned to my own mind. My books would save me. In another world, I was a king. I could fly. I could conquer anyone, anything. I retreated even further into the confines of my mind.

He told me to go wait. I could not even look at him as I walked with my head hung low. He walked to grandpa's place, and I prayed he would stay there.

My parents' room was immediately to the left of the back door of our trailer. I put my school bag down in the other room that I shared with Steve and our sister, Mary. Then I went to his room and waited.

Having already wished for death to take me, I studied the wall, waiting. I wanted to tell him, wanted with every fiber to hug him. I knew he loved me; he showed me all the time, even with the beatings. They were tokens of how much he loved me. The words were always there: "Daddy, I love you. Daddy help me, I can't make him stop, please."

They never made it past my lips. The door banged open and he walked in. The sight of me sitting there seemed to enrage him further. I saw only hatred as he told me how disgusted he was with my behavior. I felt the pain of his love with every blow of his fist. He was going to show me what it was like. This is what it felt like to be beaten. He was mistaken, as I already knew and welcomed the pain.

Out of breath, he threw the leather belt on the bed and told me to get out of his sight. This was no easy task as the hallway went through my room, the kitchen and the living room. I sat at the desk and did my homework. Steve said nothing, only did the same as always. Mary was at grandpa's house. I envied her, hated her, and at the same time was grateful.

The tears streamed down silently as I wrote out my spelling words. My butt hurt, and my head was exploding. I felt it come again, the rage. My hand snapped the pencil. I sighed quietly as I placed it with the other broken pencils. I remembered the book I was reading, and once again, I disappeared into my fantasy world.

Mom came home while he was fixing dinner. They talked as they always did about their days. When we called to dinner, my mother asked me to look at her. I raised my hand fearing she would come down on me, too.

The shrill in her voice scared me, "What happened to you? Who did this to you?" My mind was blank. How could she not know what I had done? My silence was the only answer.

Frozen that is the only word that comes to mind to describe the state. My anger had caused this, my rage. I looked across the table my brother in the same frozen state too. I did not know if he could discern what it was about, they were yelling. I could not. We were both still frozen. I was vaguely aware that tears were running down Steve's cheeks. I looked into his eyes and knew his fear.

This was not over, and now my anger would cause him pain. He was scared, both for me and for himself. The yelling grew louder and yet I could not move. I could not run. I wanted to protect him, to shield him somehow.

WHAM! Upside his head came our father's hand. I saw it and felt the ricochet off the back of the chair. What had I done? The tears then came, flowing down my face. We got up and scurried into our room, the frozen state broken by the command to leave.

I crawled onto my bed, and Steve climbed into the top bunk. Silently the tears fell. In my head, I screamed that I was sorry. I heard nothing but the raised voice, of my mother and the swearing of my father, followed by the breaking of dishes. The trailer rocked on its cinder blocks. I prayed for death again. If I was gone then there would be no more trouble…no more screaming…no more hurt…no more pain…no more tears.

Again, we trudged down to the barn the following day. The cool, crisp morning promised to be a sunny day. Saucy whinnied as I approached her stall with some hay. Looking around to make sure Steve was not around. I slipped some of the oats in her trough, too. I pet her face as she munched.

We said nothing as we headed back toward the trailer. Do you ever get that knot in the pit in your stomach when you know you have done something wrong? I lived that way for years.

One of two things happens while you are living in this hell. You are either constantly contemplating death, or running away. However, you are equally afraid to do either one. The normalcy of your reality becomes your comfort. After all, it is only tears and pain. What does not kill you does make you stronger.

The real fear behind all of this is someone, anyone, finding out. On one hand, I wanted, and even wished for the hero. They can save you, curing your ills. Then they talk of family. You blood is all you really have; if they let you down, you are lost.

"You fell off a fence. You are a walking klutz anyway so no one will question this," my mom said as she drove me to school.

"Okay." Fresh tears slid down my cheeks.

"I love you, Sarah, and your dad does too." The car door slammed behind me. The rage was boiling just beneath the surface.

~Thursday~

This was my favorite day of the week at school. We went to the library today. I was able to get a new book for the week. I read often, as it was my haven from the reality of my life. I waited impatiently, as the clock seemed to tick, slower than usual. I knew which book I was going to get. I had been waiting for two weeks to rent it from the library: *Greek Myths and Legends*. The pages filled with magical far away lands, where gods and goddesses ruled the world. They were my new heroes; I wanted to be like them.

I was almost home. We stood in line, clutching my new possession as if it could cure cancer. I made it through the questions. God bless her, Mrs. Devereaux asked twice. I made it through the long stares, and the teachers congregating with each other during recess. I even kicked a grand slam in the kickball game.

No worries here, just your average kid playing on a fence. See, I am still normal. I can still function. All is right with the world.

After we got back to class, it was an hour of free writing and art. Then I have to go home. I could be free then to curl up with my book of wonderful heroes. Why in the hell were we still in the library? I looked around and noted that the whole class was in line. We were ready. Where was the teacher? I looked around and then I saw her sitting on the librarian's desk, having a conference. While their voices remained low, the teachers kept casting strange looks in my direction. Then the class was looking at my eyes. They could not possibly be doing that, as I looked away. Then back again, yes. They were talking about me; she actually pointed at me.

The rage boiled again, so close to the surface. Dangerously close, my mind became red. A fierce beast was growling in my chest. Dear god, were they laughing? The growling got louder, and the pressing confines of the library closed in on me. I refused to let them laugh at me, I screamed, DAMN THEM!

"My FATHER DID IT, OKAY!" I screamed, the fire shooting the words from my mouth like lightening. My eyes glowed with a ferocious anger.

"NO!" my mind screamed. The beast had come out again. I was doomed. I hung my head as the tears refreshed. I had done the unthinkable. I had gone outside the family. I was doomed, sold to the gypsies for sure now.

After all, of the emotion I know I felt a sense of relief flood through me. Perhaps I could endure because now it might stop. Hope. That was what I felt then: hope. I sat at my desk back in the classroom thinking it probably did not happen. No, it could not have possibly. I had imagined it, a dream. I was convinced that it was not real until the classroom door opened and a man in a uniform was standing there.

My carefully built illusion came crumbling down. Mrs. Devereaux called my name; excused from class I made my way toward the officer. I took my things and walked toward the man in uniform. The walk seemed a lot longer than normal. I wished it were over. I held out my hands for the handcuffs. He looked down at me, kindness in his eyes as he offered to carry my book bag.

I vaguely remembered the conversation with the officer. I know I willed myself not to speak. "Just get through this," I prayed. "Then I can go home."

Home.

I am strangely comforted in the reality of this life. The fact it was not normal never occurred to me.

I was in my grandmother's house, waiting. Grandma said I was not allowed to go home. I was frightened Dad wasn't home yet. Mom was there, but she was talking with Grandma. I sat in the living room with one of my favorite books: *Aesop's Fables*.

That's when I heard the car pull up. I scrambled to the living room window to see a squad car! My father was in the back. Grandpa had pulled in first with Uncle Joey. The cops had my father, and they had brought him home.

I wanted to run out to him and apologize, explain how they made me tell. It was my teacher's fault he was there. I was so scared but I wanted him to know that it would be all right.

I wasn't allowed. We stayed the night at our grandparent's house, and then went to school the following day. When I got home from school on Friday, I hurried into the house put my stuff down. Steve and I did our chores. We made that trailer shine. He always liked that. Scrubbing and cleaning all afternoon, we made sure his favorite drink was ready and dinner working. I tried to make it perfect. I even did my homework so when he asked I could hand it over proudly. This will fix everything, I thought.

The car pulled in and he came through the gate. Thump! Thump! He pounded up the stairs. The door opened and he came in, walking down the hall toward the kitchen. I stood ready to tell him, to say I loved him. He looked around at all the hard work we had done and the dinner on the stove. Then he looked at me.

"What is this?" He said in that soft tone that made me shake as he motioned to the stove.

"I…I made dinner." I stammered in a small voice. Then I saw it again, the hatred in his eyes. His voice cut through me as he told me to get out of his sight again. Fearful of the backhand that usually followed, I scurried to my room. Steve was asked to stay as I heard him slam pots and pans, swearing.

THE STONE PEOPLE

The tears ran again, fresh. My anger had dissipated, but the hurt had not diminished. I was the bad child still, and now I had done worse. I had betrayed him. I had betrayed my family, and my home. I was no Achilles or Thor. I was a broken child.

~Saturday~

"Sarah, go get Grandpa some twigs." Grandpa said. I went to my task enthusiastically as a kid in a candy store. It was a new thing to be a part of burn day. I stood next to my grandfather as he made the flame grow with each new piece of shrubbery tossed into the fire. I remember being mesmerized by the flames themselves.

My grandfather was able to reach within the flame without scorching himself. I was in awe of this. We stood silently together watching the burning. After a while he spoke.

"Did you know, Sarah, we are of the Stone People?" His face never turned and his eyes were fixated upon the flames. I watched him reach into the barrel once more and pull his arm out without a scratch on it.

"The Stone People, Grandpa?" I asked quizzically. His answer was silence as he reached in again and adjusted some twigs. I will never forget that day.

"Yes, the Stone People." he said again. My eyes grew wide wondering how he wasn't burned.

"You, too, are of the Stone people. Reach into the fire." I wanted to, but I was scared. I looked up at my grandfather. He said nothing and smiled. Slowly, I put my arm up and inched toward the fire.

I was lost in a trance, and then the fire was warm. I felt the flames lick my skin. I closed my fist around a particular flame and pulled my arm back out of the fire. Grandpa chuckled and began putting more branches and shrubbery in the barrel. I felt connected at that moment as I bent to help him stoke the fire. We burned all the refuse and headed back to the house for lunch.

Life is made up of moments that lead us to where we are today. That moment of reaching into the fire was a turning point. I felt stronger, more solid somehow. The home life would slow down and the beatings would be less.

Something changed within me; a source of strength had changed the way I looked and felt.

The beatings were less, trading the physical for the verbal and emotional battering. Not only from my father but more from myself. The molestation at the hand of my Uncle Rodney became less as well until one day it stopped completely. The new game of verbal warfare was not my strong point, but my brother picked it up quite well. Lonely and scared I sought attention through other means.

Performing, dangerous stunts on my bicycle, eating dog biscuits and talking to myself were just a few. I welcomed the feeling of humiliation and guilt as if they were the plates in my armor. I wore them as a badge and attempted to teach others something as well. This is how I perceived love, friendship and people.

That Saturday was the greatest moment I can remember. Not only did I get to burn things, but also I learned something new: someone in my family, a man, could love me with no expectations and no hurtful manipulations. The Stone People…I was one of them.

Chapter Two: Waking up to Reality

It is very early this Saturday morning. The server just brought a fresh pot of coffee. IHOP is one of the few restaurants I know that supplies you with a pot of coffee at each table. That is where I am, and it is where I have been spending the last few months on my days off to write. I come here because it gives me a state of neutrality. Memories of my life that I have shelved, or stuffed are surfacing. Years I spent refusing to go there in my head. That is what freedom from drinking and drugs can get you old memories. The coffee tastes good; this time I am trying it with Splenda. My dad likes it this way now. Since the diabetes, he and mom have changed their diets.

It is strange to remember something from over twenty years ago. The clear head I possess today is the only way to see it with such understanding. I spent the last twenty years blaming my father for what he did, which in my mind was everything. Today I see it differently; as I believe, we both had a part in everything that we did. The other members of the family had their own paths. My parents lived their life in accordance with what they knew. I walked my path the same way.

Steve is a grown man now, living in the small town of Vacaville with his two kids and wife. Mary is facing her own demons, but in a different state. She, like my parents and grandparents moved to Oregon. Thirty years of age shows you that life goes on, and people continue to live and flourish. Why now? Why this story? I find myself realizing that my dream, MY dream has been to write. I placed myself in the hands of my creator. He has placed me here in this restaurant writing. Of course, this was not an overnight choice. Rather, it took about fifteen years to develop.

I am thirty, working at a production plant, living in Arizona. My life took a drastic change about four months ago.

I quit drinking.

Truthfully, I had done that before. I know that it sounds trivial in the eyes of a person who can handle their liquor. Four months ago, I knew that I needed to stop drinking, but it had not worked before. Nothing I did ever seem to work. I found myself kneeling at the couch in the second bedroom of the apartment that I shared with the woman I had lived with for the past ten years. Looking back, I was just as crazy as I was if I had been on a binge.

On my knees in that dingy apartment, I was planning my will and my suicide. That is where desperation takes me: planning the end. My wife walked into the room and asked me what I was doing. I knew that I had to tell her the truth. Another part of me wanted to blame and hurt her for me being there on my knees. I told her, and that is when she suggested that I try attending a meeting. I rolled my eyes, saying, "Yeah that will help, because it had before…not."

I was fighting change still. I needed something. My relationship was drowning, my job was unfulfilling, my heart hurt, and I hated looking in the mirror. Pain was not my enemy; it showed me that I was still alive. I decided that I would go to a meeting one more time, but if it was as unhealthy as I was then I was gone.

At that time, I figured that if God existed then he would show me what I needed to do. I prayed for a way to live that did not leave me on my knees, contemplating suicide. Fear has always been a driving force in my life, and that moment as no different. Anger is the mask I wear when I am afraid.

The meeting was starting in ten minutes. I grabbed the keys and left. The place was in old downtown. It turned out that it was a candlelight meeting. I was thankful for that, because that meant that they could not see my face. There were people there that I had never seen before. The meeting was nothing as I had experienced either. A woman spoke to me, offering me information on another meeting, a woman's meeting. The strangest thing about all of them is that they really wanted to help.

I met several women over the next few weeks. They were healthy, sober women that were determined to stay that way by following a few simple suggestions, one of which was to carry the message of hope. There was life available to any that wished to live.

The biggest change in my life was the difference in my thinking. I knew that my emotional rock bottom was what propelled me to go to that meeting. I wanted to learn how to live, how to be a productive member of society. I also wanted to know how to love my wife, how to be happy at work, happy at home, and happy with myself overall. Those thoughts provided me with the motivation to find the freedom I so desired.

There is a woman that saved my life; her name is Elma. She is my sponsor, my friend, my mirror. She is constantly saying odd things to me like: "That's what we do Sarah, we have crises that are tens. To other people they aren't that huge, but we make them huge. We have a disease, a disease of perception."

I listen to her, sometimes finding myself mulling over the words she chooses. Disease of perception? I thought I was an alcoholic, a drug addict. That is an illness, I know now. I am sick, but perceptions? What the hell does that mean?

I looked it up, and found, "The process, act, or faculty of perceiving." Funny, in any definition I have ever given in my days of going to school, I most certainly was not allowed to use the root word in the definition. I searched further. The psychological definition is "Recognition and interpretation of sensory stimuli based chiefly on memory. The neurological processes by which such recognition and interpretation are affected."

Now this interested me. Interpreting my life based on sensory stimuli, using my brain I affect a memory. What? Sounding intelligent, being intelligent are two different things. I have spent my life trying to sound intelligent, learning enough to make others think I was smart and capable. Disease of perception; that is my problem. What I see is not necessarily the truth of what really happened. Okay, so now I have re-evaluated my life. No, wait. That is making a simple thought into a crisis.

My perceptions of my childhood aren't always what they appeared to be in my mind. That is the reality. What I remember is not how it happened, and sometimes it wasn't the perceived hatred I felt. Instead my own inadequacies and fear were what ruled my interpretations.

Chapter Three: Perceptions, Then the Truth

I remember being seventeen, when my life took a turn down the rebellious path. I began sneaking out of the house, pushing my truck down the street so that the sound did not wake my father. I still feared him, but I began to see that being stuck here would not help me see the world and experience what my deepest desires were. After all, being gay was considered a deviant behavior in the eyes of my family.

That year I spent time with Christine and Allison, in hotels and fields. They were lovers. I wanted only to be with them to soak up anything I could about lesbians. I had only just found out that I was bisexual, and then came to fall hard for an older woman. That led me to owning my homosexuality.

Knowing a thing and living it are two different thoughts. I did not know how to live gay. All I knew was what my parents and family said; faggots were evil, a term to denote weakness. The subject of women being gay was not discussed, unless it was to say the other bad word: dyke. This term meant you wanted to be a man and lie with women, without the operation. Rudimentary thinking, yes, combined with the penthouse magazines my parents had in their bedroom. I clung to it as my formal education on being gay. The women who I called my friends were a continuation of that education. They faced many hardships during that year. Their parents found out and forbid them to see each other. Their answer was to run away together. They found reality a week or two later when they called me for help.

I watched them from the sidelines, growing up and learning to live in this world being who they were. Allison and I became closer as we shared a common bond of truth. There were times in my life that I told lies to navigate my way through everything. The times I was honest the results were amazing. They asked for money of which I had a little. I gave them forty dollars, and then they were gone.

I remember standing in front of my parent's house watching them drive away in Allison's yellow Mazda truck. I felt bad for them having to live on the run. They wanted to be together and forsake everyone that cared for them to do so. I saw the romantic side of that, but another part emerged where I saw the foolishness of the decision. They did not have jobs, a roof over their head or even the support of their families. The choice they made was going to be a hard road to walk.

It was then that I realized that I could not do that. Running away as an option, I reserved for a last resort. Then I saw the manifestation of the truth of it, that there was nothing glamorous or freeing. There are moments in life that define your character; that was one of them.

I went back inside and told my parents what had happened. I also told them I would not be seeing Allison and Christine again. Ironically, that relieved them. I think that for them it was less temptation for me to go "that way."

I withdrew more than I realized, yet in other ways I became more outspoken. Extremes, black and white…that was how I lived. I became the pursuer. My last year of high school brought many changes in my life.

I tried to get the hottest chick in school to want to be my girlfriend. I also became closer with my best friend Phillip as we discovered we were gay together. I drove to school from Dixon, wore what I wanted to wear, did my homework, talked to no one, and overall just lived I my head. I could not wait for my graduation, because then I would be free from school. I will not forget that look on my father's face afterwards. He told me congratulations, and then said he did not think I would make it. I took it to mean he did not think I could.

Going back now with the knowledge of my disease of perception, I can see that he feared I would not make it because of the way I was living. I drank everyday and tried to have sex every chance I could. I was selfish in behaviors and actions. I pulled further into the world I created in my head. I blamed him for my behavior, reasoning that if he had not been hurtful then I would not be this way. If he had not wanted me then he should not have married my mom. I was rebelling against the empty, shameful way I felt from being molested. I could not differentiate from the real perpetrator and my father. He caught almost all of the blame. The truth was that I was sick, scared and running.

My eighteenth birthday was coming soon. I knew exactly what I wanted to do. I was going to walk into a store, buy a lottery ticket and a pack of Marlboro's. This was my gift to myself. The smokes were because I could. The lottery ticket was another perpetuation of the fantasy that money could fix my problems. I would leave this godforsaken place and be free. For the most part, it worked out that way; I bought the ticket and the smokes. I proudly handed over my ID when carded and lit up as soon as I walked out of the store.

My family was throwing the party this weekend, on Saturday. They all were coming to celebrate the first grandchild having her milestone birthday.

"Time to get up! Happy Birthday Sarah, baby! We have to clean the house for company." That was my mom's greeting as I sat up that Saturday morning. My father was sitting on the couch reading his paper and having his morning coffee.

"Get the hell up! We can't be sleeping all damned day." That was my morning wake up. I did not hear him chuckle as he spoke. All I heard was the disdain in his voice. I went to the bathroom to wash my face and brush my teeth. I smiled then, knowing that I was now an adult. I was free, and he could not touch me anymore.

I thought of my grandpa then, the burn day, and the times that we had conversations together. I always came away with a bit of knowledge through his stories. He had talked about a dog collar one day. We were on his porch a few months prior, and he was saying something about a leash and collar, something to do with holding back. I did not quite get the meaning of what he was saying. He looked at me, and then I think for the first time directly spoke.

"Sometimes it's parents that hold onto their children. I think your father is putting a leash on you so that you cannot go far, and your grandma and I do not think that is right. You have to know this so that you can break free, too." He turned back to gazing at the road that ran in front of his farm. I said nothing, instantly defending him in my head. Then I took the source. I looked at my grandfather. Implicitly I trusted him with my life. I never felt like I was not part of his family just because his son was not my biological father. It was another lesson within a lesson. My father had always told me that blood was thicker than water. No one would care or love me as my family would.

Words I had not truly understood or heeded. Not until much later in life. I took his words literally. I was not his blood. I must be less than. It was another moment that defined my actions for the next ten months.

The rage that boiled within me in the third grade was there in my chest. Truth was it had never left, only laid dormant through endless stuffing. I was still afraid to let it go. Something changed so much that I became hurtful, even menacing towards my parents, my siblings, and especially Mary. I saw confirmation of what my grandfather said in the past and the present. I vowed not let it enter in my future. I became bolder in my advances toward women, openly looking at them. He did not agree with homosexuality so I became outspoken about gay rights. Pushing for acceptance and restitution.

I used my size to conquer weaker, smaller adversaries. I let my anger fuel my passion to fly away. My father became my reason to be stronger, faster, better than anyone did. In reality, I wanted to best him, beat him at his own game. I would be somebody, because he thought I could not.

I came out of the bathroom, retrieved a cup of coffee, then took my smokes and went outside to smoke my first cigarette. It felt good doing what he did not want me to do. Cigarettes were only one of those things that made me feel a part of something, a group. We cleaned the house and spent the afternoon cooking.

In my family, there is a definite reason to cook; parties, celebrations, holidays, milestones all provided the reasons for a country family to get together. My father was a legend in our family for his recipes. The meat rolls were a favorite among all of us, as were the deviled eggs. I hated deviled eggs. I did not like the way soft eggs felt in my mouth, with soft chunks. I equated it to eating puking. I always gagged when he posed the egg question.

"So…Sarah, You want to have one?" he would ask.

"No thanks, Dad. I don't like deviled eggs." usually followed with a grimace to show my disgust.

"You should try it before you say that you don't like something." My mom's opinion chimed in. That was the standard for any food a kid did not want to eat. How do you know if you do not like something unless you try it? It was always the same argument. Truth was I had tried it. I did not like his potato salad. Steve and I used to bury it in the backyard as children. The eggs in that were the same. I did not like the filling for deviled eggs; I had tried that too.

It did not seem to matter everyone else liked the eggs. There must be something wrong with me. Even Steve now liked the damn deviled eggs. Of course, it had been ten years since we buried the potato salad when we lived on Grape Street.

"I don't get it, Sarah, I think dad's deviled eggs are the bomb," Steve said as he ate a spoonful of the filling.

"Well that's great, more for you! I don't like them, I have never liked them, and I don't want any!" I yelled as I stalked out of the room. Another boy's moment, they were in cahoots again. I heard them laughing as I left to get my smokes and head outside. Slipping the pack into my pocket, I walked back into the kitchen to retrieve my soda. Let them have their fun eating puke.

"Just try one," Dad said. I turned around from the fridge and he was holding one in his hand. If I ate it, then he would leave me alone. I would puke it all up, too. I saw the scenario playing out in my mind. I did not want to do that. I was sure he would get mad. I tried to reason with him.

"No, thank you Dad. Really, I have tried it before and I do not like them. I do not like whipped cream either. Okay?" my voice wavered at the end. I sounded like a child instead of an adult. He smiled at me then. I though he would not force me to eat it. He could not conceive of that, right. I was wrong.

"When did you try my deviled eggs?" he pressed on. I thought quickly; my eyes were focused on the deviled egg he held in his hand. The only thing I could do to avoid being force-fed was to have a date, a party, a time when I had tried it. I could not remember anything. I was slipping away into a terrible place; he was forcing me to do it again. I did not want to. I told him no. I shook my head no. I said I did not like it. Why did he have to make me to do this? Why would no one help me? I was alone, and my father's face was gone. I only saw my uncle. In the playroom of my grandmother's house. Tinker toys were scattered about the floor. He had opened his pants, pointed at his dick, smiling. I opened my mouth to take his awful organ in my mouth, hating the smell of his musky sweat and welcoming it all at the same time.

I must have looked horrible because my mother was yelling. "What the hell are you doing, Gerry?" I was back in my parents' kitchen, only my father was not holding a deviled egg. He had a can of whipped cream. I felt disgusting, dirty, and horrible. I looked around as if I did not know where I was.

"She said she didn't like whipped cream. What? She ate the deviled egg?" I looked at my father as my mother looked at me. I did? I do not remember eating one but it was not in his hand. The plate had one egg missing in the circle. Oh god! I did, and I could taste the filling in my mouth. I started to gag.

"Oh Jesus! Do not be a wuss. You ate it fine…Fuck!" He yelled as I pushed through him and my mom to puke in the trash can. Now I had done it; he was mad. My mom was yelling and Steve was laughing. Mary was watching the whole scene from the dining room. My Father was laughing now. I was horrified. My mom was asking me a question. I did not understand her.

"Did you like the egg? Your dad really does make good eggs; I don't understand why you don't like them."

She had her hands on her hips as she spoke. My dad was laughing, still holding the whipped cream. I walked back towards the fridge. I was going to exit into the living room, then go through the hallway to the bathroom. The taste in my mouth was awful, as egg, puke, and copper did not mix well. My dad stopped me and spun me around toward him. I backed up involuntarily until I was against the fridge.

"Here, I'll make the taste go away," he said as he tipped the can up to spray into my mouth. I gripped the fridge, terrified. The look on my mom's face was strange.

"What the hell is the matter with you, Sarah? It's only whipped cream for crying out loud!" I started to panic; feeling like the room was closing in again. I did not want to go away again.

"Please, no. I don't want any," I whimpered in my small, whiny voice. I felt the tears on my cheeks. This seemed to irritate them more. I was fighting not to leave again. I just wanted to go outside. They were yelling, laughing, telling me that it was good. They all liked it.

"Come here Steve," my dad said as he turned toward him. I felt the room coming to normal.

"Watch your brother, he loves it," Dad said. Steve tilted back his head and opened his mouth while Dad squirted whipped cream. Steve smiled and attempted to get more. He acted as if he was happy. Dad squirted a lot and some landed on his chin. Steve laughed and Dad said something about getting it all. He turned toward Mary then, "Do you like whipped cream?" Mary said yes and ran over to get some. Dad squirted some in her mouth. They were all smiling. Then he turned toward Mom and she opened her mouth. He spoke soft to her, lovingly. I knew it was something sexual. They did that; I loved that about him. He loved our mom with utter devotion.

The tears were streaming now. They all looked so happy, having whipped cream and laughing. I was on the outside again, looking at my family. They never really needed me I could see that now. I was just a burden, a non-lover of whipped cream. Dad turned back to me.

"See, its okay. We all did it. Now it's your turn," and as he moved toward me I became scared again. Then all of them started talking to me. Telling me it was okay, that dad was not going to hurt me. They had no idea that I was afraid of not being a part them, more than I was afraid of him. I always knew he loved me, but I just did not know how to show him. Trust was not easy. I made myself do it, relax my throat and think of something else. Something I loved, like coca-cola. I could swallow that. They all smiled as I said okay. I tilted my head back and waited for the whipped cream to come. I was shaking, but I knew that more than anything I just wanted to be accepted as one of them.

After it was all done, my dad turned from and spoke quietly with my mom. Steve was smiling and Mary was asking for more. He raised his voice then. It did not matter what I did; he was still angry. My mother turned toward me then.

"I don't understand you, Sarah. Your father would never hurt you. You act as you are going to be beaten at every turn. Why don't you just grow up and accept that he is your father." The she turned back toward him. I left the kitchen and went outside to smoke and cry. Sitting on the gazebo bench, I cried. Sitting there I was torn between not being apart of my family and feeling the shame of the past. Who were they? Who was I? Why did I not fit in here…? Anywhere.

The next hour I spent preparing for my big day. I sat there unsure of what to do next. Not wanting to get into trouble, I just walked through on autopilot. Someone would ask me to do something I did it. My mother looked at me, "Sarah." I waited for the next command but one did not come. I kept my head down. I felt her hand raise my chin.

"Look at me, there is no reason to be sad. This is your day. Why don't you try to be a part of it? We love you and we are all working very hard to make this day special. The least you could do is act as if you are excited. You are 18 years old! That is a special age, a milestone." she was smiling at me. I smiled in return, guilt ridden making everyone feel bad for making my birthday special. I acted as if, that was my safety net. Pretending I could do, I lived that way for years.

"Happy birthday, my oldest daughter, my first born." she was getting nostalgic again. She hugged me, and told me that she loved me. Then she went to do something else. People started to arrive, the usual routine. Hellos all around then the men sat down to the T.V. and the women converged in the kitchen to talk. The kids found the room to play in usually with the video games or computer. Everyone wished me happy birthday as I smiled and hugged him or her one by one.

The present ceremony for birthdays does not change. The family comes over bringing presents. They get set on a table for the dreaded opening of gifts. The birthday chair is placed near the table facing the audience of the givers.

The birthday person or I sit down in the chair. Everyone else gathers around waiting for the ceremony to begin. In this case, the party was at my parent's house. The backyard resembled a small Zen garden for their relaxation. The pond with the waterfall made a nice background noise. The table sat near my parent's room sliding glass door. The spa was on the opposite end.

Being that May was not a particularly cool month, my Dad turned on the misters. The family seemed very happy, except for my parents. I thought it was originally the deviled egg; whip cream moment. I was starting to feel the excitement despite the obvious center of attention. I hated and loved it, never really sure what was to become of the situation.

I glanced at the table, trying to guess what my presents were and my excitement fell. I saw mostly cards there and three individually wrapped presents. My mom looked at me, "Why are you disappointed?" she asked.

"I am not, just curious." I told her quietly. My father overheard the conversation. "You should be grateful you even had a birthday. Instead of disappointed in the size of your gifts." I flinched at his words. They cut to the core. I was disappointed that I did not have many gifts. I did not know how he could see that. He always knew what I was thinking. Maddening it was that I would defend a lie just to prove him wrong.

The family had quieted down, I realized suddenly. That meant they could hear our conversation. My grandfather spoke,

"That's enough Gerry," he said. That was all he said my father stopped speaking. I could still feel the glare of his stare and I retreated further into my head. They were agitated, both of them. It only intensified when the family arrived. When I was not doing something for the party then I was wrong. Their words echoing an argument we had earlier.

"You are unbelievable! Selfish, ungrateful and disrespectful." he used those words. I did not know I was those things. I could not see it, later I would come to understand these are my defects in my character. I was afraid of him, under everything there was fear. I was so close to freedom. I was scared of the real world but impatient for it to get here. Sitting in that chair waiting to receive my gifts, doubt crept into my head. Maybe they could not wait either. That is why there were mostly cards.

The first gift was a brand new golf bag. I was excited on the outside. Uncle Don and Aunt Lana had purchased this because I showed an interest in Golf. I was not interested in the mechanics of the game. I wanted to have something with my father that was ours. He liked to play golf. I thought if I liked it too then he would like me. That seemed moot now. Still, I thanked them, and it was a nice bag.

My mother handed me a card, from my Aunt Tina and family. I thanked them before I opened the envelope. A card decorated with hills and a cartoon sun. It read about growing older, growing up and living your dreams. The card also had a check for one hundred dollars. My mouth fell open, and I looked at my Aunt Tina.

"Wow! Thank you so much." I stammered. They smiled and said to enjoy it. I did not understand but smiled and put the card down. I was always unsure of the protocol when opening gifts. How long do you spend on each one? Is it rude to set one down, looking for the next? My father seemed to think that was exactly what I was doing. Again, my grandfather told him to be quiet. I was beginning to feel that pit in my stomach.

The third and fourth cards held money too. A couple of hundred dollars was sitting in my hands. I began to panic. Surely the fatherly tone my grandfather used would come back to hurt me when they left. I did not understand why so many had given me money. That was a lot of money. I was planning on community college and a job after high school.

My mind reeled, almost three hundred dollars sat next to my new golf bag. They family looked strange in my mind, I felt awkward. That is when it hit me, a light bulb.

I was moving out. I was being thrown out, more likely. That is why I had so much money. That had to be it; they could not stand me anymore, or my craziness. My mother's side of the family was too prevalent, as my father would put it.

Shit. Oh, shit! I was not ready, I did not know where to go, what to do… My mind swam and the tears started to form. I realized in that moment how little I meant to them. They could not protect me from the abusers, themselves they had to cut their losses. That hurt.

It had been a tough year, I remembered worse. My face shown how distraught I was.

"Are you all right?" My mom asked as she put the next gift in front of me. This two-gift set was from her and dad. It was large and square.

"Yeah I am okay." I said quietly. I looked at the gift. I was afraid to open it, to see what it might be. I hoped it was not a suitcase. I tore open the wrappings my worst fear realized. A two-piece luggage set. The tears were refreshed and began to fall down my face. I did not look happy. I looked scared and distraught. My mother was about to say something but instead did not.

Not wanting to look ungrateful, I mumbled a thank you. Although I know it did not sound grateful at all, my parents looked confused. The pit in my stomach was huge. I looked at the kids that sat together. I wondered if I would ever see them again. I did not recognize my mother speaking at first.

"This is from your grandparents, Sarah." I took the card she offered hurriedly. I did not think my grandparents would condone this act. I had already made up my mind to walk to the farm. I looked at them, and saw them smiling. They looked excited.

"Thank you, grandma and grandpa." I said quietly.

"Open it, Sarah." grandma said excitedly.

The whole family leaned forward, eagerly awaiting my farewell gift. I took a deep breath and opened the envelope. My brow furrowed as I read. Only one line was written on the cover of the card:

Expand your horizons!

Great I thought not only did they support this idea but tried to be positive. Fresh tears escaped from my eyes. The envelope registered something else inside. I pulled it open and found a plane ticket. My heart fell. I read the destination, Paris, France.

"Oh my god!" I exclaimed. I almost crapped in my pants. All the stress left, the foreboding went away though the pit remained. I was in shock at the plane ticket in my hand. My mind slowly began connecting the dots.

Eloise. I was going to see Eloise. My best friend from freshman year in high school. We were inseparable then, since communicating through letters and phone calls. I got up and hugged my grandparents hard. The tears were running down my cheeks as I thanked them repeatedly. I sat back down; the shock wearing off my whole body sagged.

"Are you all right?" my mom asked. I just shook my head unable to speak. The pit shortly forgotten revived itself in full force when my father spoke next.

"Why were you upset before, you looked like you wanted to cry? Are you disappointed?"

I attempted to get a grip on myself before I spoke.

"I thought… You were going to kick me out of the house."

The family laughed. I looked up at the sudden noise. My father was not laughing; my mother had her hands on her hips. Her eyes spoke volumes. She was hurt, confused and angry. My dad looked perplexed as well his eyes masked by his sunglasses. My grandmother saw the unspoken tension between my parents and me, she tried to make light of the situation.

It made perfect sense to me that they were going to kick me out of the house. We had just argued about my inability to care about anyone else but myself. They did not know what to do with me; they obviously hated me and would be better off without me living there. I tried to explain that again.

"Well, I opened my presents and almost everyone had given me money. There was a lot of money. I did not understand. I figured that everyone was helping me on my way out. When I opened the luggage and the check from mom and dad, it made more sense that I was leaving. I didn't know."

They all laughed again, at least some did. Others looked shocked that I came to that conclusion. Years later, my mom would ask me about my birthday. Again, I would explain the logic in my thinking. She would get upset again, hurt. Then she said something profound. At least it was profound to me.

"You just don't get it, Sarah. You made your father and I look like ogres or something. How could you do that to us?"

My standard answer came without thought, "I don't know. I am sorry mom."

Even then, my perception in reality seemed skewed. They were good parents; I knew that in my heart. I never showed it, continuing to live in fear. Instead, I showed you a witty person with charisma. I stood in the face of adversity and said fuck you.

I did not do any of the events that seniors enjoyed. The class trip, cut day, or free periods. I worked hard on my grades and lived for the day I could leave for Paris. There I would live my life. Forever

Chapter Four: Finding Myself

Looking back I remember the inability to do anything right. The eyes of judgment that were my father's seemed to haunt my waking moments. He would joke about this in his way.

"When I die, Sarah I want you to have my ashes." I was, admittedly, shocked that he thought of me as the keeper of his ashes.

"I want them kept in an urn on your fireplace mantle, or wherever in your home. I want you to put eyes on my urn so that I can watch you forever." The thought of my father in an urn on my mantle or even my bedroom, he suggested laughingly later, was horrid. Always watching, always judging.

The thought stayed with me to adulthood. Sometimes in moments of clarity, I felt comforted that he would be with me always. Then there were other times that the thought of his urn in my house wrought anxiety. He would know all and judge all. I found myself listing his frailty's to calm my racing thoughts. He is only a man. Human. To the core of his bones, he was human.

He is not my god anymore.

I was an adult now. Free to make my own living, my own choices. I was naïve enough to believe in fairy tales of love, prestige and fame. Drinking gave me that courage I lacked. The drive to succeed. I wanted his happiness in my own world.

I knew nothing about getting that happiness. I only had my past. Sex. That was how you gained love. I became a slut. Willingly giving my body to any that could grant the kind of love I needed. They didn't even have to profess love. I took less and made believe it was real. The illusion of Oz. Perpetuated by the man behind the curtain. My three friends to help cosign my bullshit along the way.

Alcohol, fear, and my fantasy world.

I walked in fear masked by anger. I convinced myself so well that I was unaware that I was afraid. I wore anger as my battle armor. No one would ever get close enough to hurt me again. I was intimidating, threatening, manipulative and running. The engine was ran by my anger, feeling less than was the octane booster. I found a new way to beat them. Become one of them.

My yellow brick road was to be laid brick by painstaking brick with my own hands. The mortar each experience, painful memory, and degrading moment of my life. I was eighteen, a world traveler and the promise of a future before me. I came home to a disappointed family having spent all the money they gave me for the trip. The tokens of presents I brought home seemed to be not of the quality they expected.

They wanted to talk about my future. Where did I want to go, to be did I have any plans?

"Your father and I won't be able to send you to college." My mother said. She seemed genuinely sad about this. I didn't want her to be sad at my not getting to college. I figured that they had given me life so I could pay for my own school.

"That's okay, I didn't expect you both to pay for college. I can get a job, and attend a community college. Can I still live here though? It would save me a lot of money." The adult in me was beginning to show. I think that's why they found hope in the faith that maybe I was growing up, finally.

Life was smooth for a month. Things began to change. I knew I was gay. Thankfully my family didn't. I began to feel something different. The pull to be with a woman was overwhelming. I still had no clue on how to talk to one, let alone become girlfriends. I looked for help in books. I rented them from the city library. I found fictional books about women who loved women. They were a big help. Quite the fairy tale for the homosexual side of the world.

Jack n the box hired me a few weeks after I got home. The job was simple enough and I excelled at every station I worked. My anger was not an issue. At least I thought I had it under control. In the walk in freezer where we put away the stock I found hitting boxes of frozen fries helped my emotional outbursts. When the rush was on, I was in top form. In the fast paced environment of fast food I could multi-task fantastically.

I was on my way to the realm of Adulthood. I found that when I was working and going to school, my movements were tracked less by the wicked witch of the east. I felt freedom. I lived at home, paid no rent. I worked and went to school. I spent the whole of my childhood in fear. In this new world I was any character in a book I read. Thor, Zeus, or Daphne that's how I lived.

I met several people but the ones that stick close in my memory are those that affected my life. There was the older woman, Theresa. The plump woman who said she was my friend. Then there were the two I idolized because they had found each other, Christine and Allison.

Theresa was an enigma to me, thirty something working the grill. The way she looked, carried herself there was a confidence. Then the moments when she spoke were deliberant thought out word for word. This intrigued me because I couldn't, my thoughts ran through my brain bypassing the filtering device and straight out my mouth. This would be my downfall for many years.

The obsession I had for her company was overwhelming. I lied to my parents to spend the night at my aunt's then lied to her because I had a date. A ruse that spun me out of control to get to the ultimate moment.

"You keep looking at your watch, do you have to be somewhere?" Theresa asked me from the opposite side of the couch. I couldn't sit anywhere but two cushions away. I looked at the clock above the fireplace again. I had fifteen minutes until my aunt would be expecting me home.

"I have to be home in fifteen minutes." was all I could say.

Her response would keep me in a constant fantasy for six months.

"I can get you off in fifteen minutes." she said calmly.

Fear ran through my body, "I don't want you to touch me." I said quickly. Instantly I regretted the words. She took me home, to my aunt's house. She was waiting in the garage with the lights off.

I had missed my opportunity, but my mind was whirling. The conversation was short and to the point but kept me wondering. I wasn't drinking anymore and the fear to connect to another person was paralyzing.

"Sarah, I don't know what's going on, but you lied to me. You lied to your father." My aunt said.

"I know but he would kill me if he knew I had a date with a woman. I thought you would be okay with it." I said hastily. The truth was I didn't think I would get caught.

"I want you to promise me that before you go through with this, that you at least try the other side. Give it a chance your just confused." My aunt wouldn't let this go, so I promised. What she didn't know was that I had spent nine years with the other side. All it gave me was a bitter taste of love, trust and family. I hated all of them. I would follow the one thing they warned me about, my heart.

My time with Theresa was short, a lesson that we both had to walk through. I didn't know anything about her or her past. I just felt, that was enough. Reality came knocking on the door soon enough. Her ex partner of nine years came to her work, sizing me up. Tried to fight with me but somehow I wasn't threatened. I didn't know her past, nor had I asked any questions. My libido did the talking. I knew that I didn't want a triangle of chaos. We stopped talking slowly. I never saw her again after I was fired for my temper.

School presented more opportunities for me to embrace my orientation. I met a woman that I fell hard for, the epitome of what society called perfect. Blond, almost six feet, piercing blue eyes, feminine, and of course big boobs. I learned from the last encounter and asked her if she was involved. She told me no, a lie. The lessons that followed were instrumental in my life.

After three weeks of chasing her she brought her girlfriend to meet me at the college. I was devastated but didn't let them see it, little by little I learned to not trust. Man or woman they all were deceitful. Allison and I came to trust each other in a silent way that bonded our friendship. It was another lesson on the path of love that left me emotionally bankrupt.

My parents were right again and how that irritated my sense of rebellion.

"No one outside this family will ever love you as we do, Sarah. Your family is all that you have, remember that." my father said. I constantly set out to prove him wrong. Always coming back to the door with my tail broken and bruised. The fantasy world I lived in spun me out of control. I began drinking again. This time heavily.

I continued to see Allison and Christine, though my motive was different. I just wanted to get laid. Drinking allowed me the excuse to be next to them. Hoping for a whiff of something. The drinking became more important. I was now drinking every day. Beer was a warm up, once I found hard liquor the party was nonstop.

It came to the head rather quickly, I thought no one was aware of how much I was drinking. I snuck out of the house one Friday night to meet Allison and Christine. I really thought I would get some this time in their hotel room. The Jose Cuervo and six pack of beer I asked my Uncle Terry to get for me was all that kept me company. The morning came with me unable to drive let alone function at work. I got there by my some miracle. I didn't kill anybody. In the kitchen where I had to prepare breakfast for thirty my head swam. The pots in the kitchen were the stainless steel type. They were bright. My head hurt. I vomited in the trash can. I realized that I couldn't cook let alone get everything done in an hour. I called my friend Phil. I tried to talk him into helping me but he was at a loss. Instead he drove me home.

I was fired that Monday. It was the best job I had to date then. It was gone because I got drunk. Though I lied to the boss telling her a fantastical story about witnessing an accident, being trapped at the police station that morning. Frank couldn't cover me so I was stuck but there was nothing I could do. She didn't buy it, not that I blame her it was a hell of a fish story. That was the end of yet another drinking spree.

My life was heading down the destructive path quick. I did not think anyone else noticed. I kept my job losses secret or created lies that put me in a better light. My parents didn't have a clue, or so I thought. Its an amazing thing about parents, they are always aware of something. It could be only a feeling that there is something wrong. Always, parents know what is going on in the lives of their children.

Chapter Five: Coming Out

I was eighteen, my parents and I were at a stand still. My mother had withdrawn from talking to me. My father was attempting to understand why I was the way I was. I stood in the doorway of their room. He was standing in front of me, naked. My mother was naked in bed.

By no means was this out of the ordinary. I grew up being told that it was their house, their rules. They paid the bills so they did what they wanted. Walking around the house naked was a privilege. He stood there, and exasperated he exclaimed,

"Are you doing all of these things because your gay?" The question hit me hard. I hadn't heard it said out loud before. Everything in me at that moment made sense. I was gay. That wasn't why I did the things I did. That was just another way of acting out the changes I was going through. There were really two questions in his query. I answered the most important one to him.

"Yes, I am gay."

The look on his face was not what I expected. The shock, horror, or anger didn't come. It was replaced with disappointment. He was unsure of what to say next. Then he went and climbed into bed with my mother. I stood there in there room looking at them in bed. It was something from a sitcom and I smiled at that. It was my mother who spoke first.

"Why? What made you decide this? Are even aware of what being a lesbian means? What did I do?" Then she sighed, "Diseases, and AIDS," my mother added.

"We just want you to be happy. This choice you have made is not the way. It's going to be hard. Why do you always choose the hard way?" my mother asked, though it seemed she didn't really expect an answer.

I stood there, a feeling welling up inside me. I wanted them to know I was happy. I wanted to show them they were wrong. It just wasn't their version of happy. That didn't make it wrong, did it?

I sat at the kitchen table listening to their conversation. The yelling had stopped. At least for the moment. I don't know what they were arguing about, I just felt it had to do with me, again. The rage was close again, boiling near the surface of eruption. They couldn't possibly understand anything I had gone through. The last six months were pure hell. The booze was the only salvation I had, I could forget for a while.

They sat down at the kitchen table with me, a defeated tone sounded through both of them. United against me they plotted how best to get rid of me, it seemed the good witch of the north fell prey to wicked witch of the east.

"She could go live with my parents." my mom started. She only looked at my father when she spoke. That was what pushed the fear aside. Talking about me as if I was a plague upon the munchkin land. The dread that filled my stomach as the reality of what she said sunk in. I would be near him. He could do anything he wanted to me, no one could stop him. I was four years old again. Praying that I would die.

I fought against the memory, I wanted to be present. For once I just wanted to be here. I saw a backyard with grass as tall as I was standing. I thought it was a jungle.

"I do not want her to live with your family." my father retorted. My head was swimming. I was walking through the jungle. I felt something tingling my arm.

"What about your parents?" my mom asked. I saw the farm, the burning barrels. Saucy the horse. I felt a sense of hope but my arm kept tingling.

"I will not pass our problems to my parents, either." He said quietly. The tingling got more intense. What was on my arm? I looked down at my arm at the kitchen table but I saw my arm at that house. A big daddy long legs was walking down toward my wrist. I froze. The spider kept walking, then it stopped sensing my fear. Then he was gone. I looked up and he was standing their smiling down at me. My Uncle Rodney. I hugged him for saving me from the jungle spider.

The talking at the table grew smaller. I was fading away again. I shouted, "NO!" in my head. I was back in my parents kitchen. They were looking at me confused. I realized that I must have spoke out loud. The rage inside was close, some had slipped out. I must regain control. I was breathing heavily. Trying to discern their mumbled voices as to what was just said.

"Therapy. We could do counseling through my work insurance." My mother said. The second time in my life I remember her mentioning therapy.

"No." was all I heard. I think he said more but I couldn't be sure. The voices were stronger but I was drifting away again. I welcomed the anger then. Basking in the waves, that could keep me in the present. It worked.

I fueled it by thinking that my parents were discussing my future. I would be dammed if I let them dictate my life a second more.

"Military." I spoke suddenly, angrily. "I will enlist in the military." They both stopped and looked at me as if they just realized I was there. That only incensed my rage.

"What branch?" my father asked.

"I don't think that's a good idea, Sarah." My mother interjected. I ignored her and looked at my father.

"Marines." I answered. The answer was easy enough. I spent the last two years watching the commercials. I envied their strength, hardness and independence. They looked like they could kill anything. Right then I wanted to kill. My parents looked at each other, unsure of what to say at the moment. I felt good. I had stumped them.

"The marines are not the best choice. Clearly you haven't thought this through." My mother began. "Crawling through dirt and mud, carrying a gun this is not you, honey. I don't think you could kill anybody." She finished then looked at my father for support. How little she knew. How much she did.

I wouldn't be talked out of this one. I made up my mind. I saw the opening for my freedom and I was going to take it, come hell or high water. I knew that I had to convince them that I was serious. I was going to enlist. I knew at that moment with or without their help. Though admittedly with their help would be preferable. Sit up. I told myself. Look them both in the eye and defend this course of action. Wait for the opportunity then hit them between the eyes.

"I can't afford college. You both are not in the position to pay for my college. I don't make enough money to move out and still go to school. The military is a great option." I started out strong. List the obvious, what you know then steer the logic so that they can draw the conclusion you want. College was a good buzz word. They have both repeatedly said that they wanted better for their children than they had. College was one of those better things.

"I can't go live somewhere else. It would only offer more of the same chaos. In the military I will be clothed, fed, housed and paid. Then I can train for a job that will get me the financial freedom I will need in the civilian world. On the job training, school and four years experience will be hard to beat at 23 years old. Then of course with the GI bill I will eligible for college on a prepaid ride." The words came easily. I was impressed with myself. If this worked I will have fooled two of the most intelligent people I have ever met. I even considered that hastily conceived that military wasn't that bad of an idea.

They sat there, contemplative. This was the test though, withstanding the stare. I never really understood why he did this then. I never could compete against the stare. Later I realized that he was looking for conviction, truth, and the ability to believe me. I couldn't pass that test before because I was usually guilty or afraid. I stared right back at him without flinching. He knew I was right. I felt triumphant in that moment. It wouldn't be until years later that I only had done exactly what he had always wanted. I took imitative for my life, myself and my actions.

Anger had become the fuel that ran my engine of escape. I used it to intimidate others, convince them of my character and keep them away so that I couldn't be hurt. I was angry at that moment but then a new feeling emerged. I was better than him. I wouldn't be him no matter what life threw at me. They wouldn't ever fight over me again because I wouldn't be there to cause it. Instead I would be a marine. Harder, stronger, faster, better. The good witch of the north may have been persuaded by the wicked witch of the east but I found the wizard and teleported the hell out of munchkin land.

"The marines is not a good idea." my father said. "If the military is really your choice then I would think that you would consider the options, more carefully." He had found a loose chink in my chain.

"I don't see how, I like the marines. The military can offer me what I need to succeed as well get me the hell out of here." Nice comeback, I thought.

"The goal has never been to get rid of you, Sarah." My mother said, a sadness in her voice. "Is that what you believe? Do you really THINK that? We love you, we want the best for you. That's all we have ever wanted. We just don't understand what's going on with you. You don't talk to us, you walk around with your head down. When your father talks to you, all you can say is that you don't know. How can you…" she sighed. I felt guilty. I loved my mom, I didn't want to hurt her feelings.

"Mom, I…I am sorry. I just want to go, to live my life. That's normal, right? Its not fair to you and dad to stay here when I could be taking care of myself. Working toward my goals. That's all I really want. To be on my own. After visiting France I realized two things. One, I love to travel and see new places. Learn new things. Two, I couldn't afford to do that right now. The military will be a great opportunity to see the world on the government's dime. Not only that but they will pay me to travel, then pay me to go to school." Wow I was really impressed with myself. That was true. I did enjoy Paris, a lot. There was something different about the air. The freedom. That's what I wanted. The chance to do something different.

"I know you, Sarah. The marines are cool looking because they crawl in the dirt and mud, carry guns and swords. If you want to do something the air force will offer the same opportunities. At least their educational benefits are better." I looked at him shocked that he knew that. I realized then that he was right.

"Honey, she isn't all that off base. I don't agree with the marines, but the military will be a damn sight better than your parents or mine. She needs to branch out and find her place in the world." I couldn't believe it, he was actually defending me to my mother. It had only ever been the other way around. This wasn't going to work without my mothers approval. I knew that but he was taking care of that. My mom looked at him as only a wife can look at her husband. Her fears, joys, and hopes hung in her eyes. She was asking him a silent question. "Is this the right thing for our baby? Can I really do this? Will she be okay?" Then a hundred more questions all in the blink of an eye. It wasn't the first time I saw how much they loved each other. Nor the first time I saw how much my father loved my mother. It made me feel happy to be there. To witness that miracle of true love.

He turned toward me and said, "Your Uncle Billy went in the Navy. Uncle Rodney was in the marines. You see how screwed up he is, been in jail, assault charges, and he still lives with his mother. In the marines just train you for one thing. To kill. That's not a vocation that you can legally do in the civilian world. The Air Force, and the Navy train you for more than one job. I know that the Air Force gives the best educationally benefits. The Navy is the second. What do you think?"

I smiled then, the love that they had charged the air. I knew he was right. "I see your point. I wouldn't mind the Air Force at all. Can I still travel?"

"I don't see why not. They have bases all around the world. I will take you down to the recruiter next week. Tuesday, I can take that day off and we will see what they have to offer. Now you have some time to think this through."

"Thank you, Dad. I want to go, I think it's the best thing I can do for my future." I smiled and stood up. I felt good. I bent down and hugged my mom. "I love you, mom. I will come back you know. Its not forever." She hugged me back, hard.

"I know its not. I just worry for you. I love you, Sarah. I hope one day you will see that." Guilt again but I only smiled and said I knew.

One day I did see that she not only loved me but that both of my parents went through an emotional roller coaster raising their children. There were many times that they both sacrificed their money, time and peace to make it better for all of the family. I never saw that through my selfish eyes. They were just wrong and I was right. Nothing could make me see the truth.

The next week my father took me down to the air force recruiter. I didn't expect that they would say no, but that is exactly what happened. I was not physically up to their standards. My hopes were crushed. My father was the one who spoke, "If she was able to loose the weight and come to down to your standards would she be able to enlist?"

"If you do the work, Sarah. Come back and see me, we will get you signed up." the recruiter said.

There was a chance then. I couldn't believe it, I just had to loose some weight. The recruiter even gave us a diet plan to follow. It wasn't easy but it could be done. It was my dad that stood by me that year. Helped me with workout sessions. Even helped me to prepare the meals for the family and for myself. They were considerably less, close to a twelve hundred calorie diet.

The workout sessions, tennis, running and basketball that I was doing daily were demanding a two thousand minimum calorie diet. My mom got worried that I wasn't eating enough. I didn't have to say anything. My father would talk her through it, saying that it was what I needed in order to drop the weight. He stood by me that whole year, encouraging my successes.

I remember sometimes in the garage he would stay with me and do a workout too. I felt closer to him that year than I had in my entire life. I wasn't scared of him, we could talk, laugh even discuss difficult points. I had a father. I learned to channel the anger within me into exercising harder. I hated being made fun of, even in the loving sense my family had done for years. It wore on me, instead of becoming sullen. I went into my room and did pushups and sit ups. I had a new desire, it fueled my restoration to be better than any of them.

The year came to a close. We didn't know my body fat count but the weight had disappeared. I was in the best shape I could remember. Now it was test time. Dad and I went to the recruiter. I was nervous.

"You did really good meeting your goals, Sarah. You should be proud of yourself." my dad said. I smiled and thanked him for his help. In my head I heard none of it mattered unless the recruiter saw the progress.

"There is something else I am worried about, I think its best if we let them believe that you have a boyfriend. Just to keep all of your bases covered." The words hung in the air. I didn't see it then but he was trying. He didn't agree with the choice of being gay but he still was willing to help me achieve my goals. That was what a father was, encouraging your children even when you don't agree.

"How about Phillip? We both know him so it won't sound off base." I offered. He shook his head and said all right.

We walked into the mall where the recruiter station was, I remember thinking that I wished we had done something like this before. I missed having him apart of my life. I walked around scared and sullen. He wasn't that bad of a guy. I was proud to call him my father. Then a sadness erupted inside of me, because it was my fault that I didn't have a relationship with him before. I chose to stay stuck in my emotional pain, transferred my fear of men to my father. I hoped I would make it up to him. I would make it up to him.

We sat in that office together. I was proud, excited and eager to get to being a soldier. I wanted to make my dad proud.

The recruiter wasn't excited to see us, it seemed. We took measurements, did the weigh in then we sat down. He sat at his desk my dad and I sat opposite him in chairs.

"I see that you met your weight goal. Are you sure that you want to enter the air force? Won't your boyfriend be upset if you leave. Boot camp is a long time and a lot of relationships don't handle it well." the recruiter said. I knew all in a breath of a moment that he wasn't concerned with my relationship. He was fishing. My appearance was his sole judge, therefore he didn't want any gays in his air force. I was instantly angry as well as sad. I didn't say anything. I didn't have too.

"You talked with Phillip?" my father turned toward me, "Yes and his father is ex military. Air force as matter of fact. They are both happy for me, he knows what it entails." I answered. I knew instantly what that look meant. My father was about to nail this guy to the wall. He had a way about him that if you wanted to argue a point my father could play any side. First he let you think that he was in agreement then he 'Wham' he hit you with impossible logic. I sat up straighter in my chair.

"Well then they are aware. My daughter has done what you have asked. What is next in the enlistment process?" Go DAD!

"I am sorry, Sir. It seems that we don't have any openings at the moment. Your daughter I am afraid doesn't meet our criteria. But if something changes we will give you a call." I couldn't believe it, turned down by the military.

"You mean to tell me that she spent this last year breaking her ass to meet your goals. Dropped out of college, and followed your suggestions to be told no? I don't think so. She did everything you asked of her, now you want to cast her aside because of criteria? What criteria? There was no mention of how a person had to meet a criteria to enter the military. What bull shit is this?" I was in awe. My dad was sticking up for me, to this bigoted asshole.

"You can take your criteria and shove it. We will go next door to the Navy. Lets see what they have to say about my daughter joining the military." The recruiter said nothing.

My father motioned for me to wait in the hallway and he went and talked to the recruiter alone. Then he came out and the recruiter talked with me. I don't know what was said in that room but six days later I was on a plane headed to Chicago for Navy boot camp.

Chapter Six: Running from the Past

The waitress pours some more coffee in this early hour of the morning. The sun is almost up and my hand is cramped from putting pen to paper. It's just about time to head back to my apartment and go to sleep. I have to get up this evening to go to work. I pack up my things, pay my bill, and head out the door.

My apartment is normal compared to most apartments. We have lived here for only a year but have been in the same complex for almost six years. My name has been on a lease here for that long. I look around at the furnishings, the pictures on the wall, the dog who is excited to see his mama come home. I smile then because he loves me in a way no person could: unconditionally, and without doubt that I will always come home.

I take him for a walk, which means he runs around like crazy while I smoke another cigarette. I went to Oregon almost a year ago to visit my parents' place. My mom took me to the beach with her dogs. She described it as one of the few moments in life when you could see pure joy. We watched as the dogs ran up and down the beach.

Their heads were high, tongues hanging out of their mouths, and tails tied in knots as they ran, just to run free.

It was a beautiful sight. Watching Poet run around in the grass, stopping at every tree I saw it again. So often I miss the little moments that make life real. The thought occurred to me that I had not known such joy. That was interesting to me, and I went back through my lifetime in my mind. I thought about the moments that had happened, such as the day I exchanged vows with Michelle, the day I got the job at the production plant, the first time I picked up a year coin for sobriety, the day I held Poet for the first time, and time spent with friends.

They were good memories but not one of them moved me into a state of blissful joy. Happy? People ask you that, "Are you happy?" I think I have always answered yes, based on the proper view of happiness. To have a home, job, car, relationship in good standing, and trying to make it to retirement…is that real happiness for me? In my heart I heard no, faintly but there. My inner voice has been blocked by my need to control my environment. I have to go to work; that way there is money. Then I have to decide how to spend that money. Then there is time for the wife, the dog, and the friends.

The closest scenario I can compare it too is that video game for the PC. The Sims. Building a home, buying furniture, developing points for charisma, body, intelligence and to what end? The goal is to make more money to buy more furnishings, to make more friends and find a love interest. I excelled at the game only because I can cheat. I can also sleep with anyone I want because I make my points and relationship levels high enough. It becomes a challenge to see how many people I can get to like me enough.

This is real life. It is not a game. Points don't matter, people can hold grudges when you don't call, and money is not available at the nearest ATM with a magic number. Its not what I truly want. Its just what's available in my immediate future. Its also the environment I can manipulate and control. What is true happiness?

Each of us has our answer there. Mine was simple.

My true happiness is freedom.

Work that night was the same as it always was, frustrating and unfulfilling. I hated my job. I hated all the benefits that came with it, especially the pay. I came home and didn't like my house. I didn't like my wife. I wanted to be free. It was an awakening in my heart to see that the path was clear of obstacles, ironically ones I put there.

No one made me do any of it, I just wanted to fit in with the view of the many, which was to grow up, get a good job, find a woman to share your life with, and retire to die. This was the be-all and end-all of life as I knew it. Poet continued to run around showing me what it was like to be joyful and free. When he was done he comes up to me and sits; waiting for the scratch behind the ears.

I continued to work on my alcoholism through a program. It has continued to help me learn to live. I found a woman that saw through my walls and saw herself. She reached for me and I took her hand. It has been a hard road: the choices were simple, but still hard. Elma was my cheerleading squad. In the end it wasn't all her, I know that a God of my understanding reached me through her which is how I found the courage to be free.

Write, journal, keep putting pen to paper, those are the many things she tells me. I have been writing since I first learned the magic of putting those oversized pencils to lined paper. I didn't see how that was going to help me now. Then she pointed out the reality of writing.

"When we get it out on paper, Sarah, then we look at it. It is always different in black and white."

I put it on paper then I look at it.

I was beaten, intimidated, sexually molested, and emotionally unavailable during my childhood.

Hmm… Okay, its sounds more clinical now. Okay, so now what? Why?

I was punished as a child, severely, to include: a leather belt across the bottom, fists and open hands to the face and head, told I was stupid, asked if I was stupid, isolated from my siblings (whether in my own mind or reality), threatened with a two by four that had a nail in it, ignored, yelled at, and talked to.

Then my mind starts to turn and I watch the movies of my childhood flow across my eyes. Each and every instance, there are blank spots where I can't remember why I was in trouble, or what the circumstances were that warranted a punishment. I was not a perfect child by any stretch of the imagination. Logically, that leads to the understanding that some form of discipline was necessary. I like this process. It doesn't seem as big on paper as it did weighing on my soul.

My parents worked hard to provide for their family. I can see that now that I am older. To some degree the punishments I and my siblings received were extreme. My mind is clearer today. I remember that at those times in my life the punishments were stopped. Sometimes we were removed from the situation to give my father a chance to cool down. Through all of it God was with me, walking beside me and sometimes carrying me along the path. My parents didn't know what was happening, their view was that of a child who was suffering from panic attacks, disassociate behavior, and recklessness. I was running from my own pain of being sexually abused.

That's what I did: I carried my emotional pain like a badge of honor, using it at my whim to gain sympathy, empathy, friendship and love.

Okay that wasn't so easy to read. Still, it is the truth. Elma is always telling me that the 'HOW' of it is: honesty, open-mindedness, and willingness. I am ready to give all I have to this way of life. So I look at it in black and white. I cry as I remember the pain of indifference from my father. I am sad at the loss of a childhood that was robbed from me. I am also grateful to see the truth. I have no part in what my uncle did to me. I did not ask for it, or want his type of love. I have only the part of taking the shame and guilt with me throughout the rest of my life. My father loved me more than I saw at that time. He did do the best he could. My mother did everything in her power to provide for each of her children. My family is still my family, they are the ones that chose to still love me.

Then Elma has me do this sex inventory. That was fun. Every person I have ever slept with, whether for a time period or just once. Now I have to ask myself questions. Did I arouse jealousy, suspicion, or bitterness? Yes on all three counts in every relationship and one night stands.

The meat of the issue has yet to be revealed to me but I am lifted by the thought of willingness. I am willing to do whatever it takes to stay sober. I never want to be there again, on my knees planning my suicide, broken emotionally and unable to carry anymore. I ask God to remove the obsession to drink, and he does. I ask for the knowledge of his will for me and the power to carry it out. Direction comes and I run with it in hundreds of directions.

Then comes the reality. I must tell the story. I must see it from all the sides I can muster. I must relive these horrors of my past to give aid to those who still suffer. I must do these things lest I take them to my grave. My secrets… My secrets will lead me to drink. For me, to drink is to die.

I live in the same town a few years down the road. I have found an understanding of fellowship among these people. I carry the message of hope to the ailing alcoholic. In turn I receive the precious gift of sobriety. It is here that I sit realizing that my heart still hurts. My relationship is on the brink of a disaster, and for the life of me I can't see why.

I wrestle with the possibilities. She is no longer in love with me. Menopause is the cause. No that can't be right. I have learned. I have grown. I know that from my past that if I am upset, irritable or discontent there is something inherently wrong within me. That is my nature. Then why do I feel on the brink of collapsing in a state of alcoholic stupor without the drink?

Fear. I am scared. I don't have the luxury of picking up a drink to still my forebodings. I am a changed person and continually growing up.

I believe in love. I believe it exists within our lifetime. Not the love of fairytales and legends, but real love, that exists in couples who strive to grow spiritually, emotionally, and physically. My parents have it. The way they look at each other, support each other, dealing with faults, and even how they raised their children.

I lay in this bed next to a woman who has brought such joy to my life. She is the one I have waited for, wished for, and never knew I truly wanted. Still I am laying here scared to touch her, to reach out my hand and caress her back as we fall asleep. It's not rejection that stops me, nor is it an expectation on her part. It is my fear of really loving someone for the reason of loving who they are. Finding that thread of comfort, waking up every morning with a smile because you are still in love a month later, or even a year later. It is my fear of choosing to communicate over silence, finding the will to love again even when it gets hard, and accepting the nuances of her, even the ones I can't stand, because they are a part of who she is as a person.

F. E. A. R.

Forget Everything And Run.

That is what I do, my modus operandi as they say.

The problem with running away again is that I know where it gets me. I have been down that road. I know where it leads.

What now, then? The fear is still there. I want to overcome this, abandon it to my higher power, and at once began to outgrow it.

F. E. A. R.

Face Everything And Recover.

So I must tell everything, the truth of the secrets, realizing that this could hurt people that were involved. The codependent good daughter abhors the idea. It is not her that I am listening to now. It is the little girl sitting in a multipurpose room listening about child sexual abuse from family members and strangers, the one who was screaming to be seen. She is still here, and out there, reading this book wondering if she can heal, if she can enjoy life with the scars of her past. I am telling the truth because there is a mom and a dad out there, too. They work hard, attempt to prepare their children for the world that is often hard and cruel in it's lessons. They too suffer the horrible hardships of not knowing what is the right action, and then wrestling with guilt. Parents that have views of what their children should be only to be disappointed with the reality. They are a rare breed of people that become the role models for their children, after they grow up. I know that I have to forgive my father for the childhood I had. I also have to tell him that I was wrong. I judged, hated, lied and stole. My behaviors, and actions were a horrible way to show how much he meant to me. Through working a series of steps I came to realize I was powerless. My life was unmanageable and that I could be restored to sanity.

I called my dad to talk with him about my past. I asked his forgiveness for my harbored feelings of ill will. I explained that I had to do this to stay sober. My secrets will kill me. I told him I loved him, that he was a good father. Today I routinely talk to both of my parents. We laugh at my antics of yesteryear. Today my mother tells me that she is proud of me. It brings tears to my eyes, even now to know that they see the real me behind my curtains of pretense. They both have said that they are proud of the way I take care of myself and healed through my difficulties.

People can relate to being seventeen, I knew everything. Then I was on my own, twenty-five I realized I knew nothing. That's when I started to grow up. I called my parents more, because it turned out they did know everything.

Chapter Seven: Telling the Truth, the Whole Truth

My last few days in the civilian world were spent visiting members of the family, saying the goodbyes, and listening to last-minute life advice from every adult. I gave out hugs for the younger siblings and cousins. By this time the news of my lesbianism was spread throughout the whole family. It was another issue that was left to stand invisible. That is, until my Grandmother decided she would have a look behind the curtain.

I was sitting in the kitchen of her house in Vallejo. The familiar smell of peanut butter and homemade plum jam made me smile. Grandma was sitting down at the breakfast bar with me having coffee. We talked about the Navy, where I could go, and where she would like to visit. Then she took a breath and a small sigh came out. I felt the air change as I knew a question was brewing.

"Sarah, I want to know why you are gay. Did someone, some man hurt you to make you this way?" The room came into focus rapidly. I hadn't even realized that I wasn't fully there. On the outside I was three weeks away from being nineteen. Somewhere inside of me a dam broke and I was sitting in that multipurpose room listening to a doctor talk about stranger danger. I was screaming that someone should ask me if I was being hurt. I was three, twelve and every age between. My almost nineteen-year-old mouth spoke the words as my child inside waited with fear of a backlash.

"Yes, Grandma. I was hurt by a man, but that is not why I am gay." I sounded grown up. She was upset. I saw it as she got up abruptly and walked around the counter so that she was facing me, with only the counter between her and me.

"Who? Who hurt you? I want to know!" I have never heard my grandmother raise her voice or show anger to a child. I realized that she wanted to do something to him, the one who had hurt me. Now the child was screaming inside of me to tell her, but the adult on the outside didn't want to hurt her.

She waited. I had a moment to think.

"Well, Gram, it was your son, my Uncle Rodney."

I couldn't look at her. I didn't want to see the anger that might turn on me. I got up and was ready to bolt. Somehow she didn't get mad at me instead asking more questions.

"What did he do to you? When did this happen? Where did it happen?" I didn't expect that, but now that I had told someone I knew that I couldn't stop.

"He made me give him oral sex from when I was three till about twelve. It happened here in the rooms where I played with the Tinkertoys. It also happened when he came to baby sit us at home when Mom and Dad had to work."

I waited.

Then the unthinkable happened: he walked into the kitchen. I saw him and I went limp inside. He told me that it was our secret. No one could know. Besides they wouldn't believe me even if I did. I wanted to leave; I wanted to run out of there as fast as I could.

I don't remember what happened next. The days ran into each other. I couldn't wait to get to Friday. That was when I was leaving. That was fine for me, the further the better. No one could stop me now. I was free to never come back, and that was what I intended to do.

The day before I left for the Navy Boot Camp. My mother called me into her room. She asked me to help her make her bed. This was not an unusual request, but my hair stood on my skin as I heard her lock her bedroom door from behind.

We stood facing each other, pulling up the sheets, tucking them in the appropriate places. Pulling up the blankets and the bedspread, we place the pillows in the right spots.

"My mom called me yesterday. Did you tell her that you are gay because a man touched you?"

My thoughts were fast, the single most one was that it all came back to being gay. That wasn't the issue.

"No, actually I didn't say that. She misinterpreted the information." Technical and precise, as that was all I had. The semantics seemed to matter to me.

"Well, I can understand that; she is my mother. What did you say?"

"Grandma asked me if I was gay because a man had hurt me. I told her that I was hurt, but that it had nothing to do with my orientation. Then she wanted to know who." I took a deep breath.

"I was scared to tell her it was Rodney. I didn't want to hurt her, but it was the truth."

My mother sat down on the bed; her hands were in her lap and her head hung down. I wanted to know what she was thinking. Did she hate me?

"What did he do to you?" my mom asked.

"He made me perform oral sex on him." I answered, feeling small again. I fought to stay in the room.

She shot up then, pacing in front of her closet.

"When? Why? When did this happen?" she asked exasperatedly.

"Since I was about three until I was twelve or thirteen. The years sort of run together. I have huge blank spots. I do know it stopped right after my first period. I walked into Grandma's yard through the gate and he looked me up and down. His expression turned to one of disgust. From that point on I made sure that Steve and I were with Mary at all times. I didn't want her to go through the same thing I did."

"Did he ever touch Mary?" my mom asked, surprised.

"I don't think so; Steve and I were always with her. Whenever I couldn't find her I went looking. Steve was good at keeping an eye on her while we were there. I asked him to."

"Did he hurt Steve? How did you get Steve to do that? Did he know?"

"No. I don't think he ever realized. The first time it happened he was lying in the bed. He was so small though I doubt he remembers anything, which is lucky for him. I pulled him aside the day Rodney looked at me. I told him that no matter what happened we couldn't let Mary alone with Rodney. He asked me why and I just looked at him and said it was safer for her. He didn't ask anymore questions. Every time we went to Grandma's, Mary was always within our eyesight or that of you and Dad. I knew he would never try anything with you or Dad around." I finished. I was proud of myself. I expected my mom to see the good in that too. She just got quiet.

"Mom, I didn't tell Grandma about the other one." I said softly. I wasn't sure about any of this but it felt so good to not have to hold on to it anymore.

"What other one? This happened again?" she asked shocked.

"Well there was that summer that Cousin Scott came to visit, on Dad's side of the family? When we took Jessica back to Reno, he went with Steve, her and me? On the way back, Steve was sleeping and he did stuff." I didn't know how to tell her what he did.

"What did he do? Sarah, tell me, what happened?"

I swallowed hard and took a deep breath.

"First, he asked if I was awake, and then he asked me if I had ever French kissed before. I told him no, and he asked if I would like to try it. I told him no. Then he talked for a while and then kissed me. Afterwards he told me that he had a surprise for me. He went under the covers and took off my pants," I breathed.

"He kissed me down there. It felt different, and then it felt really good. Then he asked me to do the same to him, and I didn't want to do that. I tried to bargain with him. Then he had me do that, so I just thought of how it felt when he did it to me and then I did it back." I continued looking down, unsure of why I was embarrassed.

"Did he do anything else?" my mom asked.

"Yes. He pulled me back up and got on top of me. He…H…he put his thing inside of me and then that was it. Mom, I didn't want it too but it felt good, too." I couldn't look at her, as the pain and shame I was feeling was too much.

She didn't say anything at first. I didn't understand it then but she was realizing that I had had my first sexual experience. The fact was Scott wasn't exactly my real cousin because genetically I wasn't related to my father. We had never met Scott before and then never saw him again. I never looked at it like that. I just hated what I did to him. I didn't know how to tell my mom that it was my fault.

"Is there anything else that you should tell me?"

I had tears in my eyes when I looked up at her, "Sarah, honey you can tell me. It's okay."

"I…I didn't mean to kill him, Mom. I am sorry," I said softly, tears leaking down my face.

"What? What are you talking about?"

"We weren't supposed to know, but you know kids. We have a way of figuring out stuff. Two weeks later I think, I found out that Scott had committed suicide. I didn't mean to make him feel bad, and Grandma looked so sad. I couldn't tell anyone." I sobbed.

"Sarah, you didn't cause him to die. Its something he decided on before he ever met you. What happened sounds like it was a mutual experience, not one you were ready for but something that was wanted by both of you. Its okay." I didn't hear the soft compassion or love in her voice. I only heard that she was telling me I wanted to be molested.

"Rodney on the other hand... I don't know what to do, I can't do anything about it now. Why didn't you tell me before?" I looked at her, unsure of what to say.

"He told me not to tell. I was scared and I just wanted someone to ask, somehow see it and stop it. No one ever did." I said the steel on the edge of my voice. I felt that anger boiling again. The fear of it was not enough to hold it at bay. I hated my mother at that moment. She couldn't do anything! She did just as she had always done: nothing.

Nothing when I got two black eyes. Nothing when Dad called me stupid or worthless. Nothing when he hit us over and over again until we just became robots to do his bidding. Nothing every time Rodney looked at me, or came into play with the Tinkertoys that Steve and I always made things with. Nothing.

She was still talking, but I heard nothing.

I only knew that I could never trust her for protection. Maybe Grandma was right. Maybe she never really wanted me anyway. After all I was just a mistake she had when she was nineteen.

Thank God I was leaving for the military. I knew in that moment that if I wasn't heading for Chicago in the morning then I would have packed my bags that night and left.

Still, she was talking. I was standing near the door waiting to be told I could leave. The next day they drove me to the recruitment center in Fairfield. I hugged my dad and mom and said I loved them. In my heart I was only playing lip service. I was done with them and their rules, and their idea of family. All of it was bullshit.

Ten weeks later I was in San Diego going to A school, with my family forgotten and life spent drinking every night. I had succeeded in doing what every alcoholic and insane or deluded individual could do. I forgot with the change of the scenery, people and drink. It was there in sunny southern California that I learned what love could feel like, of course helped by extreme feelings that bordered on obsession and stalking. I learned that alcohol made me feel invincible, hard, intelligent, and sexy. I had finally arrived in the world of adulthood, complete with a neurotic, insane, and overall ill-conceived view of how the world really worked.

She was just a girl who came from another part of the world. She had hopes and dreams, goals and determination. She was everything that I thought I wanted to be, but she was still just a girl. I loved her, in my own twisted way. What I learned in that small barracks room was an awakening. In the end I got hurt, and so did she. We were young and unsure what real commitment meant, let alone what love looked like. I am forever in her debt for the experience.

My real hell was being locked in my own mind with my life spinning in memories that didn't make sense. The sensations that followed only angered me further. I retreated into the bottle so absolutely that I didn't see the destruction of my world. My mother had a nervous breakdown brought on by a thyroid condition. My father didn't understand why I felt the need to tell him I was getting married to a woman that I barely knew outside of the biblical sense. Consequently, he forbade me to call home because it upset my mother.

My teachers pulled me into countless conferences for reasons ranging from poor grades, to excessive partying and ultimately to intimidating other sailors. I was put on restrictive duty and thrived on the discipline. I became better but only because it was enough of a wake-up call. I didn't want to go back home, so I played by their rules.

After graduation I lied to my mother and grandmother so I could spend a week with my future wife before she left on deployment. Then I went home to show off my physical fitness. Of course after I had settled in to the routine of being home, my mother decided to pose the questions.

"Why is it you have to run to the other side of the world? Don't you want to be close to home?" I sighed. Once again, they failed to understand that I

THE STONE PEOPLE

didn't control where I went in the military. If Naples was where they wanted me to be then that was where I was going to go. I explained it again. My mother was still sure that I was secretly plotting to get away from the family.

It's strange, but as I look back now, I realize that I had put down that I wanted overseas duty. I did want to get away from the family. They were only trying to hold me down. I wouldn't ever have said it out loud. Truthfully she was right. I just could never tell her that.

Chapter Eight: Drowning

I started the story with an early memory, which seemed appropriate at the time. However now I find that other memories, earlier ones are coming forth as the days pass. The present is where we shall stay while we time travel to lessons earned and life lived. Living a life without drugs or alcohol is not easy when you are addicted to the pain that wreaks havoc through your life and the lives of others.

The road to recovery isn't an easy one either, many choices and changes have to be made none of which seem to come easily. It started at nineteen when I was put into rehab my the U.S. Navy. It was there I was introduced to a twelve step program. I wasn't ready then to accept my disease nor willing to make any changes to my current way of living.

I was stationed in Naples, Italy which is about an hour from Rome. There were three American Naval bases. One I lived at, another I shopped at, and the third was where I went to work. Moments of clarity and sobriety revealed a beautiful country. My only regret having not spent more time exploring its riches. Drinking was a normal part of my everyday experience, especially days off. We spent two to three days at a time playing video games and polishing off cases of beer. Chris and Gary were my drinking buddies. Lonely we found companionship in each other, talking of home and friends.

Chris was quite a bit older than both of us, had a wife and two children. They lived in the Midwest. He spent his twentieth wedding anniversary drinking with Gary and I while his wife waited for him at home. Four years is a long time to be out of the lives of your children and partner. Gary was from Chicago, only a couple of years older than I and we spent a great deal of time laughing. The time I spent with him was challenging and introspective. I found myself wanting to be with him but couldn't find the sexual drive to seduce him. I did sleep next to him on several occasions. Looking back now I know that he was uncomfortable with the situation. I used him for comfort without ever telling him why. I knew my sexual orientation was not the same but I hadn't found such comfort in a person that I was willing to compromise my own beliefs. I have always been a willing person to give a person everything I thought they wanted. Sex was just another tool to keep people near me.

My fiancé at the time was stationed in Washington state. I wrote to her everyday, telling her how I missed her touch and warmth. She was unaware of my activities for a while, but like any good victim I told her the truth. My reasons were to be honest and take my consequences, in hindsight it was to hurt her for being so far away. To show that I was capable of being a slut, if only she knew how to take care of me none of this would happen. I use guilt and manipulation to make her believe that I was doing it to protect her and I, somehow make our relationship better. I was a sick and twisted in my thinking.

My military career lasted approximately eighteen months. In the end the sick and twisted thinking became straightened out. I was asked if I was gay, and for the first time heard my father's voice. "Don't ever lie, no matter how much the truth will hurt. I want you only to be happy." It was strange to hear the words he said over and over, only this time I heard them with the compassion that he had always spoken them with. Tears streaming down my face I said yes and accepted whatever fate was to be had. Now I know that it was the first time I held true to what I knew and believed no matter what the outcome. I slept peacefully that night.

My life took several different turns over the next three weeks. I would be alone but under my terms, gaining my independence through trial and error. Eventually coming home to hardest lessons.

Seven days on a Greyhound bus found me dirty, tired and hungry. My grandmother picking me up to go home with her as I was unable to face my parents. It was the only time, in my mind, they had been proud of me and I was embarrassed to show my face. Their approval was my hearts desire. In the space of three weeks I wasn't able to hold true to what I believed. Left to identify my life through the process of drinking and drugs I continued down the same path I had left in Italy.

I worked two jobs while I was staying at the farm. I had no idea where my life was going, or which way I wanted it to go. I started to relive my past through traveling to old childhood haunts. I believe I was searching for answers, I found buried pain. It was a necessary walk because it sped me on my way to finding redemption.

It was strange to see my old school, Markham. The mountain next to it did not seem as high as I remembered. Memories of my school days haunted my steps as I walked the grounds. The sixth grade swings were still there. I learned to fly on those swings. They had taken down the jungle gym that girl had busted open her head on. The walls had looked so tall when I had been a student there. The doors that led to lessons of math and English had always felt heavy to open. I reached one door that was unlocked. I wondered if the heaviness would still be there. My hand curled around the handle, pushing it down. It swung easily, and my breath caught, the smell of chalk and blackboards filling my senses. I was rooted to the spot, my mind backed up to a lifetime ago.

All the girls in sixth grade liked Mr. Robinson. They thought he was rugged and handsome. Most of our teachers were older women or old men that wore business suits to class. Mr. Robinson wore shirts, his cuffs rolled to his elbows with blue jeans, and sometimes shorts in the summer. In addition, he had a mustache. I remember when some girl asked me if I had a crush on him. I looked horrified at the thought that she might know. Therefore, I lied,

"No. I do not. Ewww!" She just made a face and turned back around. I liked him enough as a teacher, but anything other than that I was petrified to entertain. I retreated further within my schoolwork and myself.

"Time for the assembly everyone. Please leave your books and things. Line up at the door." I had forgotten that there was an assembly. We stood in a single file line that would eventually bundle into a herd of children toward the multipurpose room. Somehow, we always made it back into a single line by the time we reached the double doors.

Most assemblies took place in the center of the room, and we all sat on the bleachers. This time it was different. They walked us into the center of the room where a police officer stood talking to a woman in a business suit. Our principal stood there talking with some teachers. It felt different, but I was not afraid. We took seats on the floor and waited. The principal instructed us to be silent and then introduced our speakers.

"Officer Thomas, the floor is yours." He motioned for her to step up. I had never seen a woman in a uniform before. I did not think anything could look so beautiful. She talked to us about the dangers of walking home alone, how to protect oneself when answering the phone, and strangers. It was some new movement coming up in American suburbia.

They called it latchkey kids, which were kids that went home from school and had their own keys to let themselves in their front doors. I did not think it was such a new thing. My brother and I had been doing it for years. I suppose that others had not. I liked watching her badge as it was shiny.

The officer then turned back towards the woman in a business suit. I think she motioned her forward.

"Now I would like to introduce you to my good friend. She is a counselor and a doctor. Dr. Johnson." The woman came forward. She was smiling at Officer Thomas. I remember thinking she was nice. I felt comfortable around her presence.

Dr. Johnson talked about another kind of danger, one I had not heard an adult speak about.

"I am here to teach you about families and inappropriate touching," she said. There was softness in her voice as she spoke.

"Sometimes those that are closest to us like to touch us," She began. "Who here likes to hug their mom and dad?" All the hands went into the air, some a bit more slowly with mine the slowest. "Right and that feels good, especially when our parents fix us a good snack," she smiled big. I saw other kids smiling as well. I was seeing a white light that was becoming brighter. I did not know what it was. All the light in the room was becoming brighter.

"That's a good feeling," she said. "I love it when my mom makes her chocolate chip cookies," admitted Officer Thomas. That got some giggles, and the woman doctor smiled.

"There is something else we should discuss," the doctor continued. "Sometimes our loved ones may touch us in a way that we don't like. This is a bad feeling. We don't like to feel bad, so we say no," the doctor said. I did not understand; I always said no. It did not work.

"It could be anyone that we know or maybe even a friend. If you feel uncomfortable when someone, like an adult, touches you then you should tell them no. Then tell another adult what happened. They will be able to help you," the doctor said.

The light was brighter now. I was thinking that she did not know what she was talking about. It did not happen that way. HE never stopped. He only asked again, and again, until I said yes, until I said I wanted too. I vaguely remember the doctor speaking after that. She was pointing to her body. She called certain parts of them something: danger zones. She said this is not ok, and that we should tell someone if this had happened to us, if it ever did.

WHY? I shouted in my brain. Why don't you, YOU just ask us? I screamed again. My mind exploded in a white light and I was gone again. I put my head down. I did not want to be there I just wanted to leave. Just ask, I yelled from within. I wanted to raise my hand into the air. I wanted to jump up and ask for help. I wanted so much for him to stop.

I could not do that again. I could not go outside the family. It was forbidden. The last time it only cost me my father, and I could not lose my family. I saw him in the back of the squad car and the hatred in his eyes. I pictured how the family had looked, at me, as if they did not like me either. Only he did. He liked what I did.

"Sarah, its time to go now," Mr. Robinson was touching my shoulder. I woke up to find the students filing into single lines again. I got up, and walked over to my class and waited.

I was back in the classroom, walking through another set of double doors. There were no students here, only the emptiness of bells in the silence. I walked through the fields where I played kickball as a kid and strolled past the eucalyptus trees where I had tried to smoke the leaves in binder paper. I smiled at the memory.

This walk down memory lane only irritated me further. I found no solace here anymore. I turned around, walked back to my car, and drove back to my grandparents' house. I lived there now since there was no military anymore. I worked two jobs and slept a lot. My grandmother was harder than I remember, and my grandfather seemed unsure of who I was and did not speak to me much.

Gone were the days of horseback riding. Gone were the afternoons when we listened to George Jones, Charlie Rich, and Paul Anka. There were no more burn days, and the stone people were simply a myth that vanished. I did not know who I was anymore. The only people I talked to seemed to be a psychic that cost my grandparents nine hundred dollars and my friend

Allison. All I had was the hobby of smoking dope in her garage while waiting for the opportunity to get out of Vacaville.

That is what I did…well, sort of. The day had finally come when my grandparents said I had to leave. My cousin needed a place to stay and he was a minor still. That left me, at twenty, old enough to fend for myself. So I moved in with Allison's husband, Brian and his parents until our apartment was ready. I needed fourteen hundred dollars to pay for my half, so I worked all the overtime I could.

I spent the next four months living with Allison and her husband, my unspoken desire for her growing more each day. My drinking became more of a necessity than a party trick, and dope allowed more friends into my life. That was when the parties got bigger. Then one night it happened.

Allison asked me if I would like her to fuck me. I was shocked. I almost choked on my cigarette. Then I said yes.

Every fantasy I had about kissing her, being close to her, it was coming true, although it was not the first woman for me. I fell in love in the military, and she had taught me about real lesbian love. The truth was I felt so lost and unloved that Allison's offer was the greatest thing I could have imagined at that moment.

She went upstairs and retrieved a vibrator she had and proceeded to use it on me. It turned out I never was very good at monitoring my menstrual cycle. I started soon after she began to have sex with me. She was upset at me, and I was ashamed and went upstairs to clean up. It was a horrible experience and I wanted to die. Then she was at my door asking me if I could please her instead.

All past shame forgotten, I jumped at the chance. This was another disaster, although I never told her that. She tasted bad. I was unsure why, but sour lemons were not the taste I expected. I went and brushed my teeth quickly. Luckily, her husband came home and her quickness to erase any signs was more important than anything.

I sat in my room while she attended to her husband. I was appalled at what had happened and ashamed of my behavior. This was not who I wanted to be. The fantasy certainly had not lived up to the reality. Now what? I went for the bottle. That was my only friend, my only solace against this failed love affair. It was yet another failure, and I got drunk instead. It didn't take long for my drinking to catch up to real life. Meaning that eventually all of the things I wanted to keep safe, came to light. Ironically, it would be my choices that left me in a state of chaos, pain, and turmoil.

    I sat in my room after work. The apartment I shared with my friend and her family was quiet. Brian and Allison were talking, and I could only guess what they were talking about: me. I sighed. It was my fault. I found that my choices led me here sitting in a room made for a teenager. I was supposed to be babysitting their son. He was asleep upstairs in the room. I wanted to masturbate. I went into Allison's room to get the vibrator she had used on me; I began to masturbate on the couch downstairs.

    I made the mistake of closing the blinds the wrong way. Brian came home early and, saw me through the blinds. My shame ignored by the slim chance that I could possibly lie my way out of it. I never saw his side of the story. What did he know anyway? His girl was sleeping with me on the side. Turns out, I did not think that one all the way through. He was a new father, and his only thought was protecting his son.

    I could not deny him that. He called me a pervert, asked me if I was some kind of weird child molester. That sent me over the edge. I could not think. I blanked on the next few days. I knew I had to leave, but I also knew that I didn't have enough money to get my own place. They stopped talking to me, and of course, Allison took her husband's side. That was a given. What now? I thought, sitting in this room. They talked quietly. I felt like I was home again. Mom and Dad were discussing just what they were going to do with me.

    I did what I knew how to do, which was to go home to the only people that wouldn't turn me away: my parents. I hated it but I had no choice. Brian tried to come at me and intimidate me further with his size. I just ran. I couldn't explain anything to him. I don't think a normal person could understand. Therefore, I buried the hatred, the fear, and the disgusting way I felt. I just kept running.

Chapter Nine: I Am a Dragon, His Dragon, Watch How I Will Soar

Constantly in my life, when things got too hard or just new, I ran. It didn't matter where. I ran to my grandparents, my own apartment, the navy, or even Italy. I was always running: running from the pain of my childhood, running from my own fears, running from the love that was right in front of me, to the horrors of my own making. They always caught up with me in the end. I got off the bus, the plane, or shut the door and they would be right there next to me laughing as if to say, "Wee, that was fun: let's do it again."

They say that our brains work to help us. We can train the way we think to react as if on instinct. The synapses in my brain fire based on the memory stimuli that I provide through experience. What if the way I react to situations is the wrong way? Who says what the wrong way is? How do I know what is real? These are the questions most of us that have walked through some type of pain attempt to avoid through compulsive behaviors of one sort or another. Drugs, drinking, eating, sex, or crime are just a few of them.

I am never satisfied as I run through life and I have sampled most of them. I agree that my brain is a muscle that needs and even craves exercise. I can't do pushups with my forehead. But I can change.

Change is good. It provides me with the opportunity to grow. I can love today. I can feel today. I can stop running today. How did I get from planning my suicide in the empty room of an apartment to freedom?

The answer is simple. I didn't say easy. I said simple. Most answers are, unless of course I am figuring an algorithm. I had to face my fears that I carried with me wherever I ran. I had to pull them out of my suitcase and lay them on the floor. Point at them and laugh, talk to them, write them down, even discuss them with a professional. All of it required one thing; an honest desire to change. I had that before I knew I was ready to give freedom a chance.

Rodney did inappropriately touch and have me touch him. He abused the relationship with his family. He did ruin my trust in a man that should have been teaching me how to build a bigger Ferris wheel with Tinkertoys. I can't change what happened in those nine years. I can't even expect an apology or an admittance of the truth. I was there. I know what happened. It is here that I must do the right thing. I must find a place to lay down the hurt and give him what he deserves.

Forgiveness.

I don't offer forgiveness because it will be better for him. I don't expect a relationship from him at any point in my life. I don't even care if he reads this book. I do care about me. I care about my life. Today I don't want to walk in anger. I don't want to carry fear of love and sex into every relationship I enter into from now till my death. I humbly submit to my higher power. I ask him for the strength to see the truth.

There was a moment of clarity while I was growing up that showed me the true villain. The powerful process of seeing "your" part in the uncomfortable spaces of life gives a different view to the situation.

I avoided my uncle at all costs while I was a teenager. I was scared of what such interaction might cost me.

It ceased to be a confrontation of what he did, getting him to admit his inappropriate behavior. Instead, I had to make a choice. The question comes in many forms, but the version I had was mine. How do I forgive a man who betrayed my trust in this unforgivable way? This a thought that I had when I faced my demons of the past.

My grandfather, Rodney's Dad, had a stroke four years before his death. It left him paralyzed from the neck down. It was at that time I saw the dynamic change on that side of the family. My grandparents were married for over fifty years. My grandmother became her husband's caretaker for the next four years. I wasn't around for that time in her life. I never saw my grandfather after his stroke. I did see him before then, sometime after I got out of the military.

He was excited to see me. I remember that he smiled and asked me many questions. I never really spent much time talking with him before. He told me that I reminded him of himself. He talked of traveling through the country, and his relationship with the road. I smiled and told him of my trip up the Interstate 5. He smiled as if he understood my reasoning.

He never actually told me he was proud of me but I could feel the love in his voice. After he died I went to California to be with my family. I chose to stay with my grandmother for the week. We spent a lot of time together, talking and laughing. She had business left to do after he was gone. I was grateful that I could be a part of her life at that time. I woke up one morning to make her a southwestern breakfast. We spent the rest of the morning walking through her gardens. She stopped every few steps to point out a plant, telling me about its life.

She stopped at one point and turned toward me. I could see that what she was about to say had nothing to do with plants.

"I want to tell you something, Sarah." She bent down to pick off an offending weed from her yellowish flower patch. I stayed silent, waiting for her to continue.

"Your grandfather talked very fondly of you. He was very proud of you, your life, and the way you persevered. He loved you very much, and thought you were a lot like him."

She had stopped speaking, the plant taking her thoughts away. The stubborn weed wasn't cooperating. I felt though, there was more that she wanted to say. She didn't. I stayed silent, then I saw an unusual flower.

"What is that one, Grandma? I have never seen anything like it." She stood up and walked over to where I had pointed.

"That's a lily. Isn't it beautiful?" she said fondly. It was indeed beautiful; the star shaped flower had a white outline with a concentration of pink that became solid toward the center of the bloom.

"I just thought you should know, about your grandfather. What do you think of these? They took a long time to bud, but now they are a gorgeous addition," my grandmother said. I smiled and told her that they were beautiful. We continued to walk as she talked about other plants, various coverings, and roses. I realized that she wasn't going to say anything else about my grandfather. We spent the rest of the afternoon together. I felt a warmth in my gut.

Later that day I took a nap. I awoke in the early evening, grabbed a cup of coffee and headed out to smoke a cigarette. I chose the side yard where Grandma's plum tree used to grow. I loved the red plum jam she made from the fruit. Smuckers never had anything on Grandma's plum jam.

It was dark outside unusual for most suburbs. It gave a spectacular view of the night sky and the quiet instilled a peace. I heard the gate from the backyard click open. I turned to see who it might be, and the peace in my gut shattered as I saw Rodney waking toward me.

"Sarah? Grandma said you might be out here smoking." I chastised myself for thinking that I wouldn't see him. After all, it was his father that had just passed away. I didn't expect the reaction I felt. I wasn't afraid. The fear was replaced by compassion for him and what he must have been going through. The armor still went up; it is automatic. He tried to speak, but faltered. I said nothing, watching my smoke curl into the night.

I watched him from behind my cigarette. It felt like a shield to keep him away. I thought it was ridiculous at that moment, like I was actually anticipating an attack or something. I forced myself to relax. I put myself in his position of having just lost his dad.

"You want a smoke?" I asked reaching for my pack of Marlboros.

"Sure, thanks," he said has he pulled one out of the pack. He relaxed at that moment, the comfort of a cigarette in his hands. I understood that feeling. He began to speak again. The words were stronger as if with each word spoken he was being given the strength to go on.

"I have been going to this church with my girlfriend. I didn't like it at first. I only went because she said I should." He laughed at that statement. I smiled, knowing full well the action of doing what someone else says because I am sleeping with them.

"I started to like it after a while. It was almost freeing. I owe you an apology, but I don't know how." He took a drag on the cigarette. I said nothing. I wasn't going to help him with this at all.

"I am sorry for anything I may have done to you. I found religion and I want to make right my relationship with you. Can you forgive me?"

I stood there, silent and brooding. If that is what an amends is then it was shit. I didn't want any part of it. In fact, since he decided to bring this up I was going to tell him exactly what he did. I was seething; the monster in my chest

THE STONE PEOPLE

had found the little girl that hides within me, and they merged to exact revenge upon the real villain.

Just as I was about to speak I saw a shadow of a smaller person emerging from the backyard. It was my cousin, Aidan, Rodney's only son. My anger hit a brick wall. I realized at that precise moment that I had a choice. Life brings within my path moments for choice. They are defining, and affect everything from that point on. My thought was I couldn't hurt my cousin. No matter what I thought of his father, his actions, or his halfhearted excuse of an apology; he was still his father.

I wanted to see the simple and undisputed truth. A God of my understanding showed me the truth. I had no amends for my Uncle, I owed him nothing. It was myself that I owed an amends. I didn't have to tear my family apart with the past. I could pray for my Uncle because he had a purpose too. My cousin deserved a father not a monster. I said nothing to Rodney about what he said. Instead I offered my condolences on his loss. Then I hugged my uncle and my cousin at the same time. I walked back into the house to be with my family.

The rest of the week passed easily. I wasn't angry anymore. I learned that compassion for a man who is sick grants me freedom from anger and hatred. That is what I deserve: freedom from the bondage of self that will bring me down into the pits of my own hell. Today I am the dragon I see in the mirror. I am the woman who is willing to say or do whatever it takes to stay free.

Dragons are creatures of myth. They grow with the imagination of the writer of such myths. They breathe fire, fly and produce magic of another world. They are still fierce, massive and strong. There is only one way to kill that dragon. Its heart is the weakest point of entry. Only the bravest knights dare to enter the breath of the dragon. They are the ones that stand firm and hold their swords and spears high. They charge into the flames and fly into the abyss of certain death to pierce this beast's heart. God did just that, he pierced my heart with love.

They heralded as heroes, saints, forever captured on the walls of caves to show the world that here stood a humble person willing to risk everything for the promise of immortality.

I am a dragon. I am the knight. I am free.

Lightning Source UK Ltd.
Milton Keynes UK
UKOW02f1920270516

275142UK00001B/48/P